Thomas,
Thank you for
serving our great
America. May our
awesome God keep
you safe wherever
you go.

Jeff & Jody Nadis
(Brooklyn's mom!)

Praise for
NO ATHEISTS IN FOXHOLES

I take great pleasure in heartily endorsing *No Atheists in Foxholes* by Chaplain Patrick McLaughlin. It is timely, heartfelt, and the perfect book for these troublesome times. From the calm and rustic Presidential retreat of Camp David to the hot, gritty sandscape of war-battered Iraq, Chaplain McLaughlin has been in a unique position to observe some of the greatest events of the past decade. With this book, juxtaposing prayer with commentary, Chaplain McLaughlin has created a handbook and a guide for not only our troops in harm's way but for all of us who seek to understand the world in which we live. If you really want to understand the core of America's greatness which is solidly based on faith, you must read this book.

—Homer Hickam, bestselling author of
We Are Not Afraid, The Keeper's Son, and *Rocket Boys*

Patrick McLaughlin's magnificent little volume, *No Atheists in Foxholes,* is full of reflections and prayers that are both insightful and profound. As he shares his journey from Camp David to Iraq, he presents us with a fascinating dialectic between his lived experiences and the reflective prayers that flow from them. The insights that emerge come from his looking at what is happening to him and those around him through the eyes of Faith. His insights almost inadvertently challenge and expand the minds and hearts of those who read them. McLaughlin has a way of connecting us together and reminding us that none of us are alone on our individual journeys. We are always a family who journey together and who are fathered and guided by God himself.

—Most Rev. Joseph W. Estabrook, D.D.
RC Bishop, Archdiocese for the Military Services, USA

Pat McLaughlin's prayers and observations are as singular as the man himself. Nowhere else will you find what this book offers—a spiritual journey from the Bush Presidential retreat to the war in Iraq. Nowhere else will you find such astonishing insight, prayers, and sermons. Pat McLaughlin and this book embody all that is noble, pure and profound about America.

—Lynne Bundesen, Author of *One Prayer at a Time* and
Adj. Professor of Spiritual Writing at Boston Theological Institute

Chaps McLaughlin is the quintessential Navy Chaplain. When we served together in USS Princeton (CG 59) in the mid-nineties I came to know and value his extraordinary gifts for bringing our crew closer to God and vice versa. He kept morale high, and that translated directly to high combat readiness. His keen wit, amiable personality, and his deep and abiding faith made those long days at sea more bearable for all of us. We all looked forward to the evening prayer—even the sailors who were not much inclined to pray found themselves drawn into Padre Pat's nightly connection with the Almighty. It was always so . . . *relevant. No Atheists in Foxholes* is Chaps McLaughlin's gift to all will read it. For those who have served in uniform, *No Atheists* will remind of the truth that we all pray when scared. For those not privileged to have served in uniform, *No Atheists* will bring a clearer understanding of the great compassion and commitment of our men and women who sacrifice so much to keep our great nation and others free—Padre Pat McLaughlin among them. And perhaps it will bring us all just a bit closer to the Lord as we pray with Chaps while reading his words.

—Gerard M. Farrell, Captain, U.S. Navy (Ret.)
former Commanding Officer, USS Princeton (CG 59)

I have known, served with, and admired Chaplain Pat McLaughlin since we sailed together on his first Navy deployment back in the early 1990's. He is a truly spiritual man who nevertheless knows how to have a good laugh, to take pleasure in the wonder of daily living life among America's warriors. Serving in USS PRINCETON (CG-59), he was called "Chaps" by the crew who learned from, frequently leaned on, and genuinely loved him.

No Atheists in Foxholes is eloquent in its honesty and clarity. It reflects Chaps McLaughlin's ability see beyond the chaos of life centered on and in combat to the spiritual heart of the American warrior ethos. He captures this essence untainted by dogma or doctrine, to let it shine through truthfully, sorrowfully, joyously, humanly.

This book is a must-experience for anyone interested in looking beyond mere reporting of combat to glimpse the souls of the human experience that is combat.

—E. J. Quinn, CAPTAIN, USN

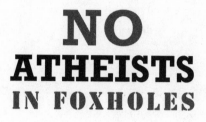

NO ATHEISTS IN FOXHOLES

NO ATHEISTS IN FOXHOLES

Prayers and Reflections from the Front

PATRICK J. MCLAUGHLIN

THOMAS NELSON
Since 1798

NASHVILLE   DALLAS   MEXICO CITY   RIO DE JANEIRO   BEIJING

Published in Nashville, Tennessee, by Thomas Nelson. Thomas Nelson is a registered trademark of Thomas Nelson, Inc.

Thomas Nelson, Inc., titles may be purchased in bulk for educational, business, fund-raising, or sales promotional use. For information, please e-mail SpecialMarkets@ThomasNelson.com.

Page Design by Casey Hooper

Library of Congress Cataloging-in-Publication Data

McLaughlin, Patrick J.
  No atheists in foxholes : reflections and prayers from the front / Patrick J. McLaughlin.
    p. cm.
  ISBN 978-0-8499-1998-5 (hardcover)
  1. Iraq War, 2003—Religious aspects—Christianity--Meditations. 2. Meditations. 3. Iraq War, 2003—Prayers and devotions. 4. Prayers. I. Title.
BV4897.W2M35 2007
277.3'083--dc22

                                                                                                    2007046671

Printed in the United States of America

08 09 10 11 QW 6 5 4 3 2 1

*With respect and admiration for those who wear the
military uniforms of the United States and their families.
They serve and sacrifice every day of the year so that
we all might enjoy freedom. To those who've given their
lives in war, may you rest at the feet of God in heaven.*

PATRICK J. MCLAUGHLIN, MDiv, STM, currently serves as an active-duty United States Navy chaplain. He has been stationed with all five branches of the armed services and has made deployments to Iraq in support of Operation Iraqi Freedom from January 2007 to February 2008 and August 2005 to March 2006. From June 2002 to June 2005, he served as the chaplain at the presidential retreat Camp David. He was ordained by the Evangelical Lutheran Church in America in 1989 and commissioned into the Navy in 1992. He currently lives in Sneads Ferry, North Carolina, with his wife, Leigh, and their children, Mariah, Jane, Megan, William, and Erin. You can find Pat online at www.pjmcbooks.com.

The ideas, thoughts, and views expressed in this book belong to the author and do not necessarily represent the views of the Department of the Navy. The text has been cleared for open publication by the Department of Defense Office of Security and Review.

CONTENTS

CONTENTS

CHILDREN DURING WAR

THE WORK OF PRAYER

PRAYING FOR THOSE BACK HOME

ECHOING THE PRAYERS OF THE SAINTS

INTRODUCTION

He that dwelleth in the secret place of the most High
shall abide under the shadow of the Almighty.
I will say of the LORD,
He is my refuge and my fortress:
my God; in him will I trust.
   —PSALM 91:1–2

As a pastor, I am called on to deliver words of hope, reassurance, and consolation. During times of war, that need is even greater as many of our nation's troops, families, and citizens take refuge in God's Word and in prayer. Psalm 91 is one of the best examples of God speaking directly to us during such difficult times.

People who serve our country come from every conceivable part of our nation, every ethnic background, and every socioeconomic status. The diversity of faith backgrounds represented in the armed forces is also staggering. In times of need, though, the collective wealth and depth of American spirituality, in combination with the Scriptures, provides our greatest resource for healing wounded souls. During times of conflict, all of us can rely on God and draw from this deep well of spiritual water.

Since January 1993 I have served as an active-duty Navy chaplain with every branch of the military. I have been shipboard with sailors, in the air with marines, on the rivers of the Midwest with the Coast Guard, with all the branches of the military at the presidential retreat Camp David, and then with marines again, this time in Iraq. I have been an ordained Lutheran pastor since May 1989, and I served churches in Virginia and North Carolina prior to entering the Navy.

I have drawn from the well of spiritual water throughout my life, but probably no more so than during the period beginning in January 2003 as the United States began serious discussions leading up to the war in Iraq. I was six months into a three-year tour as the chaplain at Camp David. It was then that I began to compose many of the prayers in this book. Less than two months after finishing my assignment at the presidential retreat, I was on the ground in Iraq with the Surgical Shock Trauma Platoon of Combat Logistics Regiment 25, part of the 2nd Marine Logistics Group out of Camp Lejeune, North Carolina. After a seven-month deployment to Iraq, I came back to North Carolina for ten months. That respite was followed by another deployment, this time for thirteen months. In the desert locations of Al Asad and Al Taqaddum, I wrote many of the reflection pieces that accompany these prayers. Over time the collection grew. At the urging of family and friends, who received these prayers and forwarded them to others via e-mail, I have put them together in the present form. I hope they give you who read these pages a glimpse into the spiritual life of those serving our country during wartime. I have met many incredible service members during my time on active duty. I have also met many of their equally dedicated families. During times of war and peace alike, many join me by drawing from the well for spiritual strength. I am humbled that God has used my experiences to uplift the spirits of our men and women in the armed forces as well as their families.

These prayers and reflections are designed to empower you to draw from the well and be a caretaker of the souls of those serving our nation, especially those whom you hold in your heart.

A TIME OF WAR

WELCOME TO CAMP DAVID

I am often asked, "How did you get to be the chaplain at Camp David?" Well . . .

Some days are more memorable than others. Some days I won't ever forget. My journey to Camp David began in the Memphis International Airport in September 2000. As I awaited a flight back to St. Louis, I received a call on my cell phone from the senior chaplain who makes assignments in the Navy. He informed me that I had been nominated by the Navy's chief of chaplains as a candidate for the chaplaincy at the presidential retreat Camp David. I had no idea that the Navy even ran the retreat, and I didn't even know the chief of chaplains. Was I willing to have my own life investigated in order to receive the necessary security clearance? Sure. After all, one of my mottos is "The worst they can do is say no." I couldn't lose a job I didn't have, and I already had a set of orders to go to the Marine Corps Recruit Depot in San Diego. I was in a no-lose situation.

In December 2000, I interviewed with the Navy staff at Camp David. At the same time, the results of the vote in Florida were at the Supreme Court. I had a good set of interviews, preached my best sermon to the congregation on Sunday (with no president in attendance), and made sure I got an embroidered sweatshirt at the gift shop. An embroidered sweatshirt would last longer than a T-shirt if this interview were the only time I would ever be at the presidential retreat.

In January 2001, I was contacted by the command at Camp David and offered the position. Many people have erroneously assumed several things about how one gets that assignment:

3

- First, I didn't know anyone in the outgoing or incoming administrations, and that wouldn't have made a difference anyway. The Navy decides who will serve as chaplain. (I had done a lot of independent duty in the Navy and was probably nominated because I had never had the chance to irritate any of the senior chaplains who sent nominees' names to the chief of chaplains!)
- Second, because of the rank of the commanding officer at Camp David, the chaplain's job is filled by a lieutenant commander. If I had come into the Navy a year later, I wouldn't have even been considered.
- Third, Camp David is a small command, and after being there for a while, I came to believe that one reason I was called there was that my experience in both the civilian world and the Navy had prepared me well to lead a small congregation. I am at home in front of a group where I know everyone by name, and I like to develop that family feeling in the church.
- Fourth, I'm certainly not the best preacher in the Chaplain Corps. In fact, the job came with a required year of postgraduate work specifically to brush up on preaching skills before I would go to Camp David.
- Fifth, as a Lutheran, I met the requirement that the nominee had to be a Protestant since the candidates for president in 2000 were Methodist (President Bush) and Southern Baptist (then vice president Gore). Besides, I enjoy meeting new people, and interviewing for the Camp David chaplaincy sounded like it would be a lot more fun than work!

As I mentioned, my assignment at Camp David actually began with postgraduate work beforehand. The Navy sent me to Andover Newton Theological School in Newton Centre, Massachusetts. Where better to send a fairly conservative Lutheran chaplain than to the Boston area and a school affiliated with both the American Baptist Church and the United Church of Christ? This move was obviously in God's hands.

Like nearly every American, I will always remember where I was on September 11, 2001: an orientation class at Andover Newton. The process of readying me for a ministry at a unique place during an unprecedented time in history began that day.

My first day on the job at Camp David was Friday, June 28, 2002. I met President Bush shortly after his arrival for the weekend. After he found out I was the new chaplain, his first question to me was "Are you any good?"—and he said it with a chuckle.

How do you answer the most powerful man in the world when he asks you if you're any good? Thank God that I'm rarely at a loss for words. The skill that landed me in trouble so many times in school would finally pay off. I simply replied, "Yes, sir. The Navy sent me here. I can hold my own." Turns out it was a good response to a president who is a very confident man.

Thus began my three-year journey as the chaplain and historian at Camp David, a journey marked by many significant events here in the United States and in places like Afghanistan and Iraq. It was a journey I made with prayer as I stood in the pulpit before President Bush, his family, and many noted members of our government on Sunday mornings as these significant events unfolded. In fact, on some sixty occasions during those three years, I stood before the congregation with my commander in chief present. Many of the prayers I shared with my family and friends during this time are in this book.

Little did I know that just six weeks after I left Camp David in June 2005, I would be serving in Iraq with the United States Marine Corps, in the very place that had dominated my thoughts and prayers while I was at Camp David. This book contains many prayers and reflections that I sent to family and friends from the sands of Iraq during my twenty months of duty (tours of seven and thirteen months, respectively).

Whether I was at Camp David or in the sands of Iraq, prayer took—and continues to take—center stage in my life. How else would I know what to say to the president in times of war or to marines, sailors, soldiers, airmen, and civilians in a war zone if I weren't consulting God on a daily basis? Without prayer, how would I know what to say to the president when he has just learned that Americans have been taken prisoner or killed in action? Without prayer, how would I know what to say to marines or soldiers who have just lost a friend in battle? Without prayer, how could I help medical teams that literally hold the balance of a person's life in their hands?

I certainly never expected to be the chaplain to the president, the First Family, the guests, and the crew at Camp David. These prayers and reflections remind me of some of those amazing days that I will never forget, days that are darkened by the clouds of war.

Prayer in Times of War

YEA, THOUGH I WALK THROUGH
THE VALLEY OF THE SHADOW OF DEATH,
I WILL FEAR NO EVIL: FOR THOU ART WITH ME.
—*Psalm 23:4*

Almighty Protector,
Freedom is not free. We are willing to pay a steep price.
We are trained for war. We pray for peace.
Danger comes from above and below, in front and behind.
We are prepared.
Fear accompanies us. We overcome. There is no other choice.
Our comrades are wounded in battle.
We will not leave them behind.
Friends die fighting valiantly. We will carry on, on their behalf.
Although I face the same, I will not fear, for thou art with me.
This is our prayer: protect us as we stand
for our nation and one another.
Amen.

6

THE BEGINNING OF A WAR

I stand in my bedroom at 10:16 p.m. on the evening of March 19, 2003, and watch as the president addresses the nation. We are now at war in Iraq. His speech is over in a matter of minutes, and I shake my head. I know that in only four days' time, on Sunday, March 23, I will be leading the worship service at Camp David. Questions immediately cross my mind. *What will I pray for during the "prayers of the people" portion of worship? What will I say during my sermon? How do I address a congregation of military members stationed there and their families, a congregation that includes the commander in chief and members of his family and staff?*

One paragraph of the president's speech stands out in my mind, and the next day I retrieve it off the Internet:

> I know that the families of our military are praying that all those who serve will return safely and soon. Millions of Americans are praying with you for the safety of your loved ones and for the protection of the innocent. For your sacrifice, you have the gratitude and respect of the American people. And you can know that our forces will be coming home as soon as their work is done.[1]

At the moment, though, I am transfixed as the television coverage begins to show bombs exploding in Baghdad. I cannot watch these pictures knowing that beneath the bombs are people. I find myself praying for people in Iraq I do not know and, simultaneously, for friends preparing for battle.

7

I leave the bedroom to go check on our two youngest children and make sure they are sleeping soundly. I go to Will's room first; he is our fourth child, who is three years old. He hasn't moved since being put to bed two hours earlier. I move quietly down the hall to the room of our fifth child, Erin, who is just sixteen months old. I open the door ever so quietly and move soundlessly across the carpet to the edge of her crib. She too is sound asleep with her angelic baby face, light blonde hair, and dinosaur footie pajamas. As I watch her breathe, I am reminded of a saying frequently heard in the military: "Others sleep under the blanket of freedom that we provide." Tears roll gently down my cheeks as I thank God for my family's safety tonight.

Now the reality of being a military chaplain hits full force. We are at war. I have known that this was coming for several months. In fact, I have seen the president at Camp David quite often since the beginning of the year. But the war is not real until I stand in my infant daughter's room and shed tears in silence. I pray again to God for wisdom.

I know that the president mentioned prayer in his address to the nation.

In the past few minutes, I have already prayed three times.

God will give me the words for Sunday's sermon.

The one thing I can do now is pray . . . for our country, for our president, for the people of Iraq, for our troops, and for a swift conclusion to this war.

In times of war, prayer is one of the only ways we can try to make sense of things as we talk with our Lord in candor, humility, hope, and desperation.

On August 26, 2005, I find myself in prayer as I depart from Marine Corps Base Camp Lejeune, North Carolina. I finished my three-year tour at Camp David two months earlier. Now it is my turn: I am on my way to Iraq. I have just said good-bye to my wife and youngest daughter, who is now nearly four years old. I find myself in quiet tears again—and I hope that none of the marines on the bus will see. Then I notice that several of them have eyes filled with tears.

We all need prayer and the protection of the Almighty.

8

Prayer for Peace

THE SOLDIER ABOVE ALL OTHER PEOPLE
PRAYS FOR PEACE, FOR HE MUST SUFFER AND BEAR
THE DEEPEST WOUNDS AND SCARS OF WAR.
—*General Douglas MacArthur*

God of All Power and Might,
Recognize us as a fallen humanity as we pray to you.
We pray for peace around the globe.
When peace is broken, the result is not glorious war,
but rather the ravages of death.
Grant that our actions may prevent war
and our wars restore peace.
Bestow patience on our ambassadors and lawmakers.
Bless the leaders of the world with wisdom.
Give our citizens, government, and military
the courage to defend the right of all people
to live a peaceful and productive life.
Watch over your quarrelsome children, Lord,
until the day of eternal peace.
Recognize us as your children, we pray.
Amen . . . and peace . . . and amen.

WELCOME TO IRAQ

An Iraqi Security Forces (ISF) soldier lies on the operating table. He has undergone two hours of abdominal surgery, and the extent of his gunshot injuries is now quite clear. He has suffered irreparable damage to major arteries; specifically, his iliac arteries have been shredded. Despite the extraordinary talents and efforts of the surgical team and thirty units of blood, the surgeons have no choice other than to pack his abdomen with gauze, apply pressure, and hope that the bleeding stops. The technique—using something called a "Bogota bag"—is a simple and ingenious way to temporarily close the abdominal cavity. An IV bag is drained and cut open along the edges to form one big sheet of heavy plastic. The opened plastic is then sewn over the gaping abdominal opening to keep the organs in the cavity and some pressure on the packed wound. Despite all the modern technology and all the training these doctors have received, this is the only way to treat such a catastrophic injury.

The lead surgeon's gown is spattered with blood. In his eyes I see a look of anger and frustration. He turns to me in the operating room, which is actually a tent, and asks, "Chaplain, do you believe in miracles?" I tell him that I do, and he adds, "You'd better start praying for one now." I detect a hint of frustration with the Almighty in his remark—as if to say, "Where is God now?"

What a way to spend your first day in Iraq . . .

I have been praying all along. I have been talking to God to keep him apprised of the situation—as if God didn't already know one of his children was in dire straits. I know by heart the story of how Jesus brought Lazarus back from the dead, stench and all. But I am not a healer. It is miracle enough for me—as one who has never seen a surgery performed, much less a wide-open abdomen—to stay for the entire procedure without even a hint of queasiness. And to me, another miracle is the dexterity and talent of the surgical team operating under such primitive conditions. Welcome to Iraq.

When this soldier came in, he was conscious and talking. The entry wound, just below his bulletproof vest on the left side, was no bigger than the end of my fingertip. I know that because I saw the doctor insert his finger into the wound. The soldier was going into shock. And now this big man—just over six feet tall and weighing somewhere in the neighborhood of 220 pounds—is a man losing the fight for his life. The Bogota bag is leaking blood around the edges. The bleeding has not stopped, and the abdominal cavity is filling with blood.

The miracle of healing, silently prayed for by everyone in the room, does not come. Blood pressure dwindles until it cannot be detected; the heart rate begins to drop and then races over and over again; a ventilator forces air in and out of his lungs. Two and one-half hours later—five hours after surgery began—the soldier loses his final earthly battle and dies.

At his side are doctors, nurses, corpsmen, and me, a Christian chaplain praying for a man who is most likely a Muslim. Tears are shed quietly. A prayer is said. His soul is commended to God's care. The tents that house the operating rooms and recovery area are now silent.

I still believe in miracles even though one was not received in this case. If I could have performed a miracle, I would have. Instead, all I could do was pray for this Iraqi soldier and for those who would follow in his footsteps to this same fate.

I find that prayer will be my constant, welcome, and needed companion in Iraq.

Prayer for a Fallen Iraqi Soldier

Almighty God,
I pray for this fallen Iraqi Security Force soldier's soul.
Perhaps he fought for freedom . . . or for a peaceful country
for his family. Or maybe his was just a much-needed job.
Today he sacrificed his life. I do not know his name,
but somewhere a mother, father, brother,
sister, wife, or child will begin to mourn.

Hear my prayer, Lord.

I pray for the doctors, nurses, and corpsmen
who tried for hours to save him.

Hear my prayer, Lord.

I pray for the sailors and marines who rushed
to donate blood in an effort to save him.

Hear my prayer, Lord.

With your gracious mercy, receive his soul. Forgive his sins.
He is a child you created. Accept him back into your arms and
make him whole. I am your child, too, and he is my brother.
This war has taken yet another of your children.

Hear my prayer, Lord.

Dry my tears. Give us peace.
Amen.

THE REST OF THE STORY

The cause of death is listed on the death certificate as homicide. That is an eye-opener. Even the military classifies this as a homicide. The real cause is war—our inability to live together in peace.

If I could perform only one miracle, it would be to bring about peace. I want to believe in that miracle.

Less than two months ago, I was in the serene beauty and well-manicured grounds of Camp David, enjoying the cool, crisp breezes of the Catoctin Mountains of Maryland. Now I sit on a wooden bench outside the Surgical Shock and Trauma units and shake my head as if I could shake off the experience of the past five hours. The heat—115 degrees—hangs heavy in the still air.

Today is Saturday, August 27, 2005. Tomorrow I will sit in church and ask God for strength to face this war and life-and-death situations like this for the next seven months.

But for now, I remember the words of the young marine who, in the dark of the night as we deplaned from Kuwait just hours earlier, said, "Welcome to Iraq. Welcome to hell."

Those were the first words I heard on the ground. After arriving on a flight from Cherry Point, North Carolina, to Bangor, Maine, to Keflavik, Iceland, to Bucharest, Romania, a planeload of marines and sailors from Combat Logistics Regiment 25 (CLR-25) and 6th Civil Affairs Group (6th CAG) unload in Kuwait. I should have known that the deployment to Iraq would be unusual. We had taken this less-than-direct route on a contracted flight aboard Miami Air International. I assume it is another illustration of the well-known military phrase *the lowest bidder*. The crews of Miami Air International are friendly and wish us well as we depart in Kuwait. After spending the night in a hot tent with sixty to seventy men, we load our seabags and packs and head for our flights into Iraq.

The second unusual twist comes with our flights to Camp Al Taqaddum in western Iraq. We are flown via C-130s piloted and crewed by the Michigan Air National Guard. I quickly learn that "one weekend a month and two weeks in the summer" doesn't apply to the National Guard. So another lesson is learned: expect the unexpected.

C-130s are hot and incredibly loud. The crew member at the back of the plane is drenched in sweat but seems to take it in stride. Getting on the plane in Kuwait and then getting off the plane in Iraq, we line up like cattle, quietly following the person in front of us. In the blackness of night, there is no rank. We just get in line. That's when I hear it. As we off-load and move away from the plane, a line of marines passes us, headed onto the plane for the journey home. A lone voice hollers out in the darkness, "Welcome to Iraq! Welcome to hell!"

Prophetic words. I show my age by muttering to the young marine in front of me, "We're not in Kansas anymore, Toto." The marine gives me a quizzical look and just keeps moving. We all keep moving.

And that is another theme in Iraq: just keep moving—hour by hour, day by day, month by month until it is time to take your place in the line of those headed home. For now, there are still another seven months until that day for heading home arrives for me.

I begin the practice of writing prayers and reflections. It is how I will deal with the months to come. Little do I know at this point that I will return to Iraq after this initial seven-month tour to spend another deployment here. Next time it won't be for seven months; it will be for an entire year. More prayers . . . more reflections . . . and somehow God will see me through.

Prayer for the World Community

YOU CANNOT SPILL A DROP OF AMERICAN BLOOD
WITHOUT SPILLING THE BLOOD OF THE WHOLE WORLD . . .
WE ARE NOT A NATION, SO MUCH AS A WORLD.
—*Herman Melville*[3]

God of All Peoples,
You created the world.
In one breath we became brothers and sisters.
You created nations thousands of years old
and nations not yet a decade old.
You created America, and people from all over the world—
brothers and sisters—have continued to flock to her shores.
When blood is spilled, it is the blood of your children.
When blood is spilled, it is the blood of brothers and sisters.
When blood is spilled, it is the blood of a nation
and the blood of the world.
Grant us understanding.
Grant us goodwill.
Grant us unity.
We pray as your children.
We pray as a nation.
We pray as a world community.
So be it and amen.

A LESSON IN FAITH FROM A MUSLIM FATHER

Shots ring out, and people in the village of Jazeera take refuge inside the courtyards and confines of their homes. Unfortunately, by late 2005, it is an event that they are accustomed to. While the village is a small place, these Iraqis are proud that until recently, their children have received an education, and they are a dignified and independent people.

Yet making a living in rural western Iraq is difficult. The ground can be unforgiving. The heat and lack of rainfall make for a short growing season. Life is made more difficult by anti-Iraqi forces that have used their village school as a shelter and as cover for some of their attacks on a local Army checkpoint. Rapid-fire bursts of AK-47 rounds are heard as the enemy moves its position away from the schoolhouse and closer to houses in the village. With no warning, a fourteen-year-old boy is shot in the chest as he plays with his six younger brothers in his backyard. The family thought they were safe inside the walled confines of their yard.

The bullet that struck this teenage boy was a stray ricochet from the gun of an insurgent who was firing at the nearby Army checkpoint. One of the first lessons of war is that a bullet has no conscience.

But I learn another lesson of war here too. When your child is shot—especially, in this country, your firstborn son—you'll do anything to save him. Within moments of the young boy's getting shot, his father braves the firefight, carries him through the dusty streets of Jazeera to the Army checkpoint, and literally hands him to an American soldier standing next to a tank. The soldier is stunned by the appearance of the father carrying his young son and instinctively takes him, a reaction to the out-thrust arms of

16

a man carrying a wounded child. The concerned father knows that the best medical care is available from the Americans, so without thinking twice he hands his son over to a total stranger, a combatant, a foreigner who does not speak Arabic. This is the father's sole hope of saving his dear son's life.

Without reservation I can say that Iraqi children are quite beautiful. Their olive skin and dark features light up when they smile. They have the deepest brown eyes you've ever seen. Unlike American children, they have a slight build and look younger than their actual age. This teenage boy is rushed to Camp Al Taqaddum by a small convoy and arrives at the Surgical Shock Trauma Platoon (SSTP) tents, accompanied by an Army medic who has already done a great job bandaging up the boy's wounds and making him as comfortable as possible in a Humvee traveling the bouncing terrain. Through the translators, the boy says that he is in no pain. After a quick examination, the attending doctor says it appears that the bullet entered the boy's side below his right armpit and exited through his right chest wall. With this type of wound, he is undoubtedly in pain, but he is determined to put on his toughest face. His toughest face to me, though, is still the angelic face of a child who should never have to suffer the ravages of a war fought by adults.

When his father handed him to the checkpoint soldier, he did so with complete faith. The soldiers at the checkpoint tried their best to tell him where they were going to take his son. The insurgents continued to send rounds in the direction of the checkpoint. The soldiers could not send the father after his son right away; they had to wait until it was safe to transport the father through a dangerous corridor of roads to get to Camp Al Taqaddum. It is almost two hours later when the father arrives at the entry checkpoint to be checked for identification and searched for any weapons. By the time he is escorted to the SSTP tents, his son is out of surgery and awake in recovery.

I greet the young boy's father before the translator has returned. In only a few words of English, he asks, "Is he okay?" I nod my head yes and lead him back to the tent serving as the recovery area. I speak less Arabic than he does English. With that affirmation and at the sight of his son alive and awake, the father lets his tears flow and begins to kiss his son's forehead and hands. He turns to me and, still not altogether composed, shows me the large bloodstain that covers the front of his shirt. Then he pulls out the handkerchief in his pocket and points to his son. Clearly, it is his son's blood

17

from when this devoted father carried him so quickly and gently to get help. I have witnessed many reunions when soldiers are returning from deployments, but this is the most beautiful reunion I have ever witnessed as the young boy smiles and is even a bit embarrassed by his father's emotions.

When the translator returns, the father is profusely thankful, and he begins to tell the translator the story of what happened. This is his oldest child, and his pride in his son is quite apparent. He tells us that he is a good boy, a hard worker on the family's small farm and diligent in school. He laments the fact that because of the insurgents, it is no longer safe to attend school in the area. He also tells us that when his son was shot, he didn't hesitate to risk not knowing where his son was going—as long as his son was with the Americans who would give him the best medical treatment available. The father explains that he has faith in our doctors and that their reputation is known all over the area. And so, without hesitation, he handed over his son—his firstborn son, his helper on the farm, his pride and joy—with complete faith and trust. The translator has explained to him who I am and what I do as the chaplain for the surgical unit. The father turns to me and says that God is good and that he knew that God and the Americans would take care of his son. He says that all of life in Iraq is in God's hands.

It does not matter that his son was prayed for by a Protestant chaplain and operated on by a Catholic surgeon and a Jewish surgeon. Those are mere details about the people who are instruments of God's hands during this time of crisis.

Here, in a war-torn country during the Islamic season of Ramadan, I am learning what living faith really is. I—a Christian chaplain—am learning from an Islamic father that faith means letting go and trusting God and other people at the absolute worst, most traumatic time of your life. I am learning that faith means risking everything to save someone you love. I am learning that faith is a blessing that comes with an unwavering belief in God, and sometimes in humanity, despite living in the midst of the worst of humanity's actions. I am learning about faith far from home and not from a book, not from another chaplain, not from a sister or brother in Christ, but from a Muslim father.

When our discussion ends, we sit down as proud fathers. He is the father of seven boys—quite a source of pride in a farming village where their help is invaluable. I tell him that I am the father of four daughters and one son. He grins and says he feels sorry for me. It is now past sunset, so he can have something to eat. We offer him a take-out plate from the mess hall, but all he accepts is some water and crackers. We sit on plastic milk crates and eat in silence. Grateful for his brave young son, grateful for skilled doctors, and grateful to God, we share this meal that is more meaningful to me than any communion table I have ever knelt at.

In less than ten minutes, he and his son board an ambulance headed to the airfield and a medevac helicopter that will take them to the hospital in Baghdad. It does not matter that neither of them has ever flown in a helicopter. I learn that faith and faith alone will see them through this entire ordeal.

I shake his hand as he boards the ambulance, and I tell him, "God bless you." He understands this, folds his hands together, points toward heaven, then points toward me. It is his way of saying the same thing to me. I have received one final blessing from this Muslim father. It is the most meaningful one I will receive during this entire deployment. I am more proud of this moment than of any of the awards I wear on my dress uniform.

Over a year later I can still picture this brave young boy and his father, and I realize that God has sent me a lesson in faith.

From the sands of Iraq, in the midst of the Al Anbar Province, I am grateful. I am blessed. I have seen what true faith means.

THOSE WHO SACRIFICE

Prayer for the Willing

IF A MAN HASN'T DISCOVERED SOMETHING
THAT HE WILL DIE FOR, HE ISN'T FIT TO LIVE.
—*Martin Luther King Jr.* [4]

Gracious Lord,
We have found that we are willing
to die for you and your message.
We pray for missionaries who have lost their lives serving you.
We pray for those at risk
because they lift up your name unashamedly.
We do not want to die, but we are willing.
All who serve in our nation's military have found things that they
are willing to die for—nation, family, friends, justice, or their
brothers and sisters in arms—and we pray that our nation's forces
and those of nations around the world may not have to die.
We do not want to die, but we are willing.
Hear our prayers for peace and unity among all of your children.
Remind us that we are your children—
of every nationality, race, creed, and color.
Give us strength to pray for our enemies
and to turn the other cheek.
Give us passion and courage to stand up
for causes worth the cost of losing our lives.
Give us compassion to know when to compromise,
negotiate, and find a way around death.
Life is not always easy or fair. People do not always
value the gift of life that you have given.
We pray because we need discernment.
We pray because the world can be a dangerous place.
We pray because we are human.
Hear us, Lord.
Amen.

THAT'S MY POLICY

So many friends and family ask me about my feelings and opinions on the war in Iraq since I am a veteran of this war. There is plenty of debate out there about why we are at war in Iraq. Should we be at war? When will the war end? Is there an exit strategy? Five or ten years down the road?

Believe me, active-duty military members discuss these issues. As you might expect, military folks are fairly conservative. We are all bound by a chain of command that stretches from the most junior private and seaman recruit all the way to the commander in chief, and I've worked with privates and presidents. That means I am not free to comment on a policy of our chain of command as a military representative no matter what the situation or policy. Gays in the military—there is an official policy. Nuclear weapons—there is an official policy. What uniform you can wear out in town—there is an official policy. The war in Iraq—there is an official policy. So don't ask me to write or record my opinion about an official policy. We all accept that, as part of serving our nation, we freely give up the right to some of our opinions while we're in uniform in order to serve the greater good. We still have rights as private citizens, but even then we are careful about what we say. We follow orders. We have to, or a combat unit could not function. You can't just choose which orders and policies to follow based on limited information or a whim. In the movie *A Few Good Men*, Jack Nicholson, playing a marine colonel, says to Tom Cruise, "Son, we follow orders, or men get killed." That is the stark truth.

I will tell you this: there is an abiding belief in most of the military that freedom is worth the cost. It is more than a belief; it is a way of life. Even

24

if it costs a life. This thought underscores what we stand for. You see, sometimes we go to places where freedom is only a thought and a dream. We deploy to places where there is freedom on a limited scale. While in those host nations, American service members have to be careful what they say and do. Freedom is not a worldwide concept. The type of freedom we enjoy in America is a lot rarer than you might expect.

As a veteran now of two tours in Iraq, I'm amazed that some Iraqis still want to fight, that some want to return to old ways that limit their freedom, that some are afraid of freedom. I often think that if we could just take each citizen of this country on a tour of America, stop at our home for a meal, and then bring them back, their perspective would change. Imagine being able to take them down the boardwalks of San Diego, California . . . drive them across the vast plains of the Midwest with the Rocky Mountains looming on the horizon . . . stop for some fried chicken and sweet iced tea at the Beacon Drive-In in Spartanburg, South Carolina . . . treat them to a Philly cheesesteak in Philly . . . stroll down the amazing sidewalks in New York City to watch ice skaters in front of Rockefeller Plaza . . . taste fresh lobster in Maine . . . sit in a rocking chair on the porch of a log cabin in the Smoky Mountains of East Tennessee . . . attend a village fish fry in Southern Illinois . . . drive across Iowa, where rows of corn stand in perfect lines as far as the eye can see . . . take one ride at Disney World . . . give them a glimpse of a Little League baseball game . . . tour a supermarket that has so many aisles of food that the mind spins . . . give them a chance to fish from the pier and walk the beaches in Naples, Florida, where I grew up . . . stop at a church or synagogue or mosque of their choice to worship.

That is a naive thought—a dream—but it is a dream that you and I get to live each day in the United States.

Stop and think about how many countries do not allow their citizens true freedom to worship, read, demonstrate, vote, travel in safety and peace, determine their own future, open a business, get an education, or obtain equal rights for women—just for starters.

I don't have all the answers to why we're in Iraq or even if we should be here. I don't know when the war will end or how. I don't know how much longer we'll be here. But we are here now. You can't undo that. Peace has to be secured now. There is really no other solution.

Why? In my opinion two very basic reasons:

Freedom.

Peace.

Children free to go to school . . . children free to pray, whether to Allah or Christ or Yahweh . . . children free to run and play . . . children free to grow up and vote . . . children—and adults—able to live with freedoms that we often take for granted. If you could see or live for a while in a place without these freedoms, you would understand.

Iraq. That's where I am now; that's where I live now. I am in a place where I don't have these freedoms. Iraqis have worked hard and risked much, including their lives, to vote and live free.

I can't go back in time. I don't make political or military policy. I don't carry a weapon. I am a chaplain, and I pray for those who would work for freedom from this day forward, those who would rather be back home with their own families and friends, those who don't want to die in a foreign country but will make that ultimate sacrifice if it is for freedom and peace.

This is the policy that I make, a pact with God and the marines, sailors, and soldiers I serve: to pray for them, to pray for peace, and to pray for their families and the families of Iraq so that we all can live and raise our children in freedom. I will go with my marines and sailors and stand with them wherever freedom is at risk. That's my own policy, one I feel is worth living and dying for. That's a lot of prayer and a lot of time deployed away from my home and family, but I'm prepared for both the prayers and the mission. That's my policy.

Prayer for Military Children

WHEN YOU COMIN' HOME, DAD?
I DON'T KNOW WHEN, BUT WE'LL GET TOGETHER THEN, SON.
—*Harry Chapin, "Cat's in the Cradle"*[5]

God of All Mercy,
May my children forgive me for all of the missed birthdays.
Help my children forgive me for all the plays,
band concerts, basketball games, and
Christmas pageants that I will have to forgo.
Console me when I read in letters about Baby's first steps,
first words, first stitches, and first date.
Let them know that I miss them more than they know.
Remind them that I will suffer through months
without their hugs and kisses.
Tell them that the videotapes and phone calls
are as close as I can be for now.
I promise to send silk pajamas from Hong Kong,
gold hoop earrings from the United Arab Emirates,
and a tiny stuffed kangaroo from Australia.
I won't forget to bring back water from the River Jordan
so that they can show their Sunday-school classes
the waters that might have baptized our Lord.
Watch over my children as I serve my country—losing time with
them and never making some of the most precious memories.
Grant that the example of my sacrifice and commitment
to my country will teach them more about me, more about
the cost of freedom, than any words I can speak.
Bless all of the children in America tonight when they pray,
"Send my daddy home soon" or "Send my mommy home soon."
Lord, I miss my children; I love them;
I commend them to your care.
Amen.

THE MILITARY LIFE

My wife, Leigh, and I are the parents of five wonderful children. Each of them was born in a different state. They are from Virginia, North Carolina, California, Illinois, and Massachusetts. Additionally, we have lived or been stationed in Rhode Island, Missouri, Maryland, and Pennsylvania. Our oldest daughter, Mariah, attended ten different schools between kindergarten and eleventh grade. Rather than attend an eleventh school in another state, she finished high school a year early and began college as a seventeen-year-old.

We have friends from all branches of the military service and the civilian sector spread across the entire country. We've attended big churches, medium-sized churches, and small country churches. Our children have been to large museums in Los Angeles, San Diego, St. Louis, Boston, and Washington DC. They have been to such amusement parks as Disneyland, Disney World, Knott's Berry Farm, Six Flags in Missouri and New Jersey, Carowinds in North Carolina, and Hersheypark in Pennsylvania. Toss in theaters, aquariums, and historical sights. They've been onboard the USS *Constitution* as I preached, attended Easter Sunrise service in Boston Harbor, and toured the White House and Camp David. Our kids are much richer for all of these varied experiences.

But our family has also experienced leaving friends and family far behind. They live through deployments, new schools, new music teachers, and new houses. The most difficult question they can be asked is "Where are you from?"

The only places my children haven't seen are overseas duty stations. The

Navy knows how expensive that move would be for a family of seven and has declined to issue us orders to these locations even though I have asked on several occasions.

When people want to know how our family has adjusted through all of these moves, I tell them it has been a whirlwind adventure requiring flexibility, and a journey filled with love and the warmth and caring of many local churches.

Military families serve just as the military member does.

They serve during peace and war.

They serve through long separations and many moves.

Pray for the family each time you stop to pray for the military member. The military man or woman cannot make this journey without the help of God, family, and friends.

A SELF-CENTERED PRAYER

*A feeling of real need is always
a good enough reason to pray.*
—HANNAH WHITALL SMITH

A friend, who is also a writer and my mentor, told me that when I write, I should write about what I know.

My wife, who knows me better than anyone except God, tells me that I write best when it comes from the heart.

So I will be honest with you . . .

Sometimes our prayers are very self-centered, and at times, that is okay.

Last night I found myself praying for peace as part of my evening prayers. The petition for peace is a constant prayer of mine. I'd like to think it is a noble prayer too.

But last night I prayed for peace so that this war would end right away. And when I say right away, I mean, by some miraculous happening, tomorrow.

That sounds noble except I prayed this so I could go home and be with my family.

You see, my wife's picture is on the screen saver of my computer on the desk next to my bed. The pictures of my five children cover the wall next to my bed so that they are the last things I see when I go to sleep at night and the very first things I gaze upon when I awake each morning.

My prayers last night were very self-centered.

I miss my family. Next to being willing to sacrifice my life, the greatest sacrifice that I make for my country and my Navy is the years—yes, years—that I have spent separated from my wife and children as part of my military service. I know many others just like me who are sacrificing unrecoverable time away from loved ones to serve for freedom's sake.

My prayers last night were self-centered, and I think that is okay. I miss and need my family, and as Hannah Smith said, "A feeling of real need is always a good enough reason to pray."

I have a real need and six of the very best reasons to pray for an end to this war.

Prayer for Military Wives

LOVE CAN BUILD A BRIDGE
BETWEEN YOUR HEART AND MINE.
—*The Judds, "Love Can Build A Bridge"*[6]

Lord,
The military speaks in terms of courage, honor,
devotion to duty, sacrifice, and commitment—
all of which are qualities of the military wife.
We thank you for wives who run households for
months on end while their husbands are deployed.
In fact, Lord, they usually things run more smoothly.
Give these wives strength to deal with pregnancy,
childbirth, colic, potty training, the first day of school,
teenagers, bills, broken-down cars, burst pipes,
lonely nights, and mothers-in-law.
Grant them the patience of Mother Teresa,
the superpowers of the Bionic Woman, and the financial
wizardry of Suze Orman so they can stretch military pay.
In short, Lord, let us recognize that the job of
a military wife would wear down even Wonder Woman!
We pray that their sacrifice and support are given more praise
than the career accomplishments of their husbands.
There are no words greater than "Thank you" and "I love you."
May we use these often with the wives of soldiers,
sailors, marines, airmen, and Coasties whether we are
at home or deployed around the world.
Love can build a bridge between our hearts. Let us see to that!
Bless all those military wives who serve and sacrifice
to support their families and our great nation.
Amen.

LETTER TO MY WIFE

11:45pm
07 Nov 2005
Camp Al Taqaddum, Iraq

Leigh,

In a prior letter you wondered whether being here has changed me. Some days it has made me darker—angrier and sadder. You would not be surprised to know that on many days I am very adept at keeping people at arm's length with a biting wit and sarcasm—and laughter.

I can't say what changes will happen long term. I hope that I will never have to be separated from you and the kids in such circumstances again.

I do know that God has sent me here for the corpsmen, nurses, doctors, marines, and patients. I know that I have been sent here to complete a full circle beginning at Camp David, coming here, and then returning back to the States. I know that completing that circle—that being an advocate for peace—may come with a price. I know that my story has meaning in a confusing war and that my story must somehow get out. It is a debt I owe God and others.

Yes, being in Iraq has changed me. It gives me a perspective that makes many worldly things seem inconsequential. It is aging me a little faster. If I were unaffected by all of the death, mutilation, and injury, though, I would be very worried about who I am.

When it is all said and done, I will want to remember it all. To not remember in some way lessens the pain and dignity of those who pass through the SSTP.

When it is all said and done, a part of my soul will be injured. If it weren't, I would have no heart. This is a very small price to pay compared to those brave children I have seen. Yes, children who never should have had to pay this heavy a price. Their souls may suffer irreparable damage. Children have no place in the SSTP!

When it is all said and done, I will finish my prayers and reflections even if it is only for our children to read and understand who their father is.

When it is finished, I want to be with you—to hold you and to be held.

Tonight I pray for peace and ask God to carry my burden and grant me a night's rest so that I will face tomorrow—another day of war—with honor, courage, and a heart ready to help those around me. If I can do that each day, I will get through all of this, and I will be changed for the better.

I love you,
Patrick

Evening Prayer for My Family

BUT AS FOR ME AND MY HOUSE,
WE WILL SERVE THE LORD.
— *Joshua 24:15*

Lord of My Family,
I thank you for each night I am able to be with my family.
I make the rounds tucking in children, telling stories,
receiving hugs and kisses, hearing prayers, and saying,
"I love you!" Beloved Winnie the Pooh, a windup musical
rabbit, soft blankets, CDs playing quietly, night-lights on—
all small trinkets of safety and security in a child's life.
They remind me of true blessings in life.
I thank you for my wife. Finally she drifts off after a day
of interpreting baby speak, picking up toys, helping with
homework and piano, driving a shuttle service,
cooking meals, and healing the boo-boos and bruises of life
with warm embraces. She reminds me of true love in life.
I even thank you for the tired family dogs sound asleep
on the hallway rugs and the cats on the end of the bed.
(How many dogs and cats this week? Three, five, or eight?)
You remind me how this family extends beyond
conventional boundaries, as does your limitless grace.
There will be nights when I am away serving my country,
and I ask you to watch over my family then.
Tonight I am grateful and content with my blessings.
So good night, Leigh. Good night, Mariah, Jane, Megan, Will,
and Erin. Good night, Junior, Salem, Winston, Mollie,
Sylvester, Figaro, Tony, Lucy, Harry, and Hermione.
Thank you and good night, Lord . . .
Lord of my family. Good night.
Amen.

COURAGE AND COMMITMENT

*This event took place during my second tour
in 1996 and exemplifies the courage,
commitment, and sacrifice military spouses exemplify.*

When the bedside phone rings at two o'clock in the morning in my home, it is never good news. My wife answers the phone, and all I hear her say is, "Yes, sir. Right here next to me . . . Yes, sir. I understand. He'll be there as quickly as he can get into his dress blues. Yes, sir. Thank you. Good-bye."

I am wide awake now as my wife explains that there has been a helicopter crash and that I need to get to work ASAP. In military terms *ASAP* means "as soon as possible." In reality it means now, if not sooner.

As I drive toward headquarters, I notice that the sky is overcast with no ambient light from the night horizon or the moon. A combination of ground fog and mist complicates flying conditions. Mist only serves to scatter what little light is available when pilots are using night-vision goggles. By 2:30 I speed into the parking lot and see the lights on in the commanding and executive officers' offices. I am greeted stoically by the commanding officer of the squadron of the two downed pilots. He immediately briefs me on the accident that happened nearly two and a half hours earlier at sea, within sight of the ship where the helicopter was to land. Search results indicate that there is no good news. Witnesses saw the crash, yet very little wreckage was found. It is as if the shallows of the Atlantic Ocean just swallowed any evidence of the helicopter and its two pilots.

As we drive to the home of one of the wives whose husband is now officially missing at sea, neither the commanding officer nor I speak of the

36

dreaded moments we will face there. At three o'clock, we ring the doorbell. She knows as she opens the door and finds a Marine officer and Navy chaplain in dress uniforms that we have bad news.

What transpires that night through tears of grief and the next few days of visits, preparations for a memorial service, the memorial service, and the funeral remind me that military wives are among some of the most courageous and committed women I know. Wives are not paid, but they serve right alongside their warrior husbands. They take care of homes, kids, bills, cars, jobs, and illnesses while separated from their deployed spouse. In worst-case scenarios, they suffer the tragic and unexpected loss of their husbands in the line of duty.

Courageous, committed, honorable, devoted to duty, and *willing to sacrifice* are terms used to describe those in uniform. Those terms apply equally to military wives. Many wives serve as the backbone for the family, a role that allows the military member to have a successful career. And so we pray for the wives of military members who epitomize courage and commitment, and we remember the words of Proverbs 31:10, 28:

Who can find a virtuous woman?
For her price is far above rubies.

Her children arise up, and call her blessed;
her husband also, and he praiseth her.

Prayer for Military Husbands

LET US NOT LOVE IN WORD, NEITHER IN TONGUE;
BUT IN DEED AND IN TRUTH.
—*1 John 3:18*

God of Many Blessings,
Thank you for the husbands
who support the careers of their military wives.
Remind them of great women like the prophet Deborah
who served God and her nation on the front lines.
Grant them knowledge of your Son, Jesus,
who was deserted in his hour of need by his disciples,
only to find that the women stayed with him.
Our nation is blessed by men who will run households,
chase kids, prepare meals, change poopy diapers,
help with homework, hold down jobs, and pray,
while their wives are called away to serve our nation.
The only constant in life is change, and as traditional roles
change, let us embrace all military spouses whose
love and fidelity make their partners' service possible.
Be with the husbands who take on
the demanding role of military spouse.
Encourage them whose love is not just in word,
but also in deed.
Bless each one today for the sacrifices he makes.
Amen.

Prayer for Parents

TELL ME AND I'LL FORGET; SHOW ME AND I MAY REMEMBER;
INVOLVE ME AND I'LL UNDERSTAND.
—Chinese proverb

Lord,
We are proud of our sons and daughters
who serve this great nation.
It seems like only yesterday that they
were learning to walk and talk.
Filling the hallway walls of our homes are pictures
outlining their lives—the most recent picture showing
them proudly wearing the uniform of their country.
We pray that our children will be guardians of peace.
We pray that our children will safeguard freedom.
We pray that our children will
bring honor to their families and country.
We pray that our children will return to us safely.
Watch over our children, O Lord, for they are a part of us.
It seems like only yesterday that they
were learning to walk and talk.
We are proud of our sons and daughters
who serve this great nation.
Amen.

WAITING FOR A LOVED ONE: THE WAR MOTHER'S FLAG

A small flag hangs in the window at a neighbor's home. The flag is a simple design: a single blue star is centered on a white background, and the flag is trimmed with red. Today, though, few people notice or even know why this flag, no bigger than a standard sheet of paper, hangs in the window. I'll gladly explain: our country is at war, and this flag hangs in the window of a mother whose son or daughter is serving in the military. Inside, the home is filled with prayer.

In the early stages of the war, a military member and chaplain arrive at a home displaying the flag. The unthinkable has happened. The mother is notified of the death of her young son—a marine, soldier, sailor, airman, or coastguardsman—killed in action in a foreign country thousands of miles away. Grief stricken, the family prepares for the impending funeral and community memorial service. Flowers, cards, and visitors with baked goods arrive at the home of the distraught family. As family members and friends arrive to express their condolences, they notice the small flag in the window. The flag no longer contains a blue star. Now the star in the center of the flag is gold. Now prayers for comfort and words of gratitude for making this sacrifice are the only consolation neighbors can offer.

American Gold Star Mothers and Blue Star Mothers of America came into being in 1917 during World War I. Army Captain Robert L. Quiesnner of

40

Ohio designed this flag to represent the service of his two sons during the war. The flag caught on, and chapters of Gold Star and Blue Star Mothers were organized around the country. American war mothers serve while they watch and wait—Blue Star Mothers with pride, apprehension, and prayer and Gold Star Mothers with pride, sacrifice, and prayer. The flag honoring the mothers of World War I flies over the United States Capitol at eleven o'clock on the eleventh day of the eleventh month—Veteran's Day. Also, the last Sunday of September is, by proclamation of the president of the United States, observed as Gold Star Mother's Day.

The War Mother's Flag was displayed prominently in homes during World War II. Some flags even displayed a combination of blue and gold stars, and some—as in the case of the Sullivan brothers of Waterloo, Iowa—sadly contained as many as five gold stars.

The War Mother's Flag was not displayed as often during the Korean War and even more rarely during the Vietnam War. However, a flag with a blue star flies in the front window of my parents' home in Naples, Florida, a home filled with pride, apprehension, and prayer. The safety of their only son and the thought of possibly losing him in war are never too far from my parents' minds.

Recently a stranger rang the doorbell of my parents' home. My mother opened the door to a woman who explained that she knew she had to pray for someone today; she just didn't know who or what her prayer was to be. The small flag with the blue star caused the stranger to stop and share her story as well as her prayers for our entire family.

We are called to pray if we ever encounter a home with a War Mother's Flag placed in the front window.

Those who watch and wait, especially mothers, are also serving in times of war.

Prayer for Brothers and Sisters

HE THAT DWELLETH IN THE SECRET PLACE OF THE MOST HIGH
SHALL ABIDE UNDER THE SHADOW OF THE ALMIGHTY . . .
A THOUSAND SHALL FALL AT THY SIDE,
AND TEN THOUSAND AT THY RIGHT HAND;
BUT IT SHALL NOT COME NIGH THEE . . .
THERE SHALL NO EVIL BEFALL THEE,
NEITHER SHALL ANY PLAGUE COME NIGH THY DWELLING.
—Psalm 91:1, 7, 10

Most High God,
Bless my brother, bless my sister,
for they serve in our nation's military.
Protect and keep them under the shadow of the Almighty.
Keep them safe in the midst of danger and chaos.
And if their comrades in arms fall at their sides,
let them carry on in their defense.
Send your angels to take charge.
Deliver them and honor their faithful service.
Pride fills my heart.
Prayers occupy my soul.
My faith is in you, O God.
Amen.

Prayer for Those Missing the Birth of a Child

WELL, I JUST HEARD THE NEWS TODAY . . .
—*by Scott Stapp, "With Arms Wide Open"*[7]

O God,
I missed the birth of my child today.
Ten fingers and ten toes I ache to count.
My baby will be months old when I return.
Deployed far from home, I received the call.
O God,
I missed the birth of my child today.
I'm confused, guilty, and proud—
Proud of my wife and proud to serve;
Guilty to have missed the blessed arrival.
Deployed far from home, I received the call.
O God,
I missed the birth of my child today.
Tears roll down my cheeks, and you see my joy and pain.
Let me return safe to my precious newborn.
Deployed far from home, I received the call.
O God,
Keep us safe.

THE BEST AMCROSS MESSAGE

The American Red Cross has helped the military in a variety of ways in times of peace and through the trials of war. One of their services to the military is verifying medical and family emergencies. Once it verifies a medical situation, the Red Cross sends a message to the service member's unit to notify him or her of the situation at home. These messages are called AMCROSS messages. Commands need the verification of the Red Cross in order to make decisions about whether or not to send a service member on emergency leave.

One of the most dreaded things sailors can hear from their division officer is "You need to go see the chaplain. He has an AMCROSS message for you."

Generally AMCROSS messages notify a service member of an illness or death of a family member. One of the most difficult jobs a chaplain has is to notify a service member of a sudden and tragic death of a loved one.

Every now and then an AMCROSS arrives for a very joyous occasion, specifically, the birth of a child. The message usually reads:

Member's wife requests notification. City Hospital, Anywhere City, FL reports birth of daughter, Jane Doe Smith, 6 pounds 15 ounces, 21 inches, 1035 EST, 09 November 2005. Mother and baby doing well.

It is rare that the chaplain gets to deliver this message. Messages of the birth of a child are often delivered by either the commanding officer or the command senior enlisted leader. When the message is delivered to a sailor

44

on a Navy ship, congratulations are announced to the entire ship over the ship's intercom. On one occasion I was asked by the sailor to notify him when the message came in since I saw all the AMCROSS messages on the ship after they had arrived in the radio division. He didn't want our ship's captain (who was not very popular with the crew) to be the one to notify him of the birth of his first child. After I notified him of the birth of his son, we had to go through the charade of notifying the captain. The sailor feigned surprise and elation, and the captain thought that he was the good guy. The captain was perhaps the only one on the ship who didn't know that I had already informed the sailor of the good news.

The last three of my five children were born while I served on active duty, but I was able to be there for their births. While the birth of a child is a joyous day, it can become, after a few hours, a depressing day for a service member who is deployed thousands of miles from home. He may have to wait as little as a few days or as much as a year until he is able to hold his child. The birth of a child is, from the military's perspective, a normal, everyday occurrence that does not warrant sending the service member home on leave from a deployment.

Now, with the advent of video teleconferences and video clips from digital cameras, the service member is able to see his newborn child in a matter of hours or days. Still, there is an aching longing to be there at such a precious time. That child may be the only child that service member will have. In that case, he has just made one of the most difficult sacrifices of his career by missing the birth—and it may not be the first milestone that he will miss.

When we thank our military personnel for their willingness to provide us with our everyday freedoms, this is another reason we do so. Some of the most important moments in their entire lives will be reported to them in a letter or an AMCROSS message. Pray today for those who will miss the birth of a child because they are serving and sacrificing for our country.

FELLOW WARRIORS

Prayer for Veterans

AND ONE WAS SAFE AND ASLEEP IN HIS BED
WHO AT THE BRIDGE WOULD BE FIRST TO FALL,
WHO THAT DAY WOULD BE LYING DEAD,
PIERCED BY A BRITISH MUSKET BALL.
—*Henry Wadsworth Longfellow in "The Midnight Ride of Paul Revere"*

Almighty God,
Washington and Grant and Eisenhower led
Troops into battle to answer the call.
For freedom some were injured and bled,
And more than a few would not return at all.
Fighting for the flag or a small piece of ground,
Military of all branches working together as one.
A braver lot of men and women have never been found
Thanks to parents—willing to send a daughter or son.
In every corner of the globe our veterans have fought
On the ground, through the air, and on the sea.
Our security at high cost they have bought
So that we can worship and speak among the free.
Bless all who wear the uniform with pride.
The Stars and Stripes will continue to fly
By the sacrifices of many who have fought and died.
We continue in their steps—traditions to occupy.
When each American is safe and asleep in his bed,
A lone soldier stands at his post.
His grandfather and father to arms have sped
To protect our great land when needed the most.
So this is our prayer to heaven above
Whether in times of war or in peace:
That every veteran would know of our love;
That one day on earth the fighting would cease.
Amen.

49

DRIVE IT LIKE YOU STOLE IT!

Most people don't realize that it would be impossible for the military to move all the supplies it needs on its convoys without the help of contracted truck drivers. Many of these truckers are employed by KBR (formerly Kellogg Brown and Root) and come from the United States.

By their own admission a majority of the drivers are Texans. That makes sense. You need to view yourself a bit larger than life to drive off every day facing possible IEDs, land mines, small arms fire, and rocket or mortar attack. Don't they say that everything is bigger in Texas? A large risk . . . A large number of Texans . . . Makes perfect sense.

But these drivers come from every region of the States.

Why on earth would anyone choose to drive a truck without all the armor of a military vehicle in a dangerous place like Iraq? To say that the drivers are a colorful bunch is an understatement. They are quick to laugh and are a close-knit community. Many of them wear T-shirts that say "Operation Iraqi Freedom—Drive It Like You Stole It!"

They like to kid about the reasons that they drive in Iraq. Fuel is free. Tires are free. There is no Department of Transportation or Highway Patrol. In reality, these drivers make pretty good money and have a chance to get ahead of bills and house payments.

Make no mistake, though. These truckers take the same risk as the marines and soldiers they drive with. They simply don't wear the uniform. In September the stories of three truckers from a base called Anaconda made the news. They were pulled from their rigs during an ambush and killed by insurgents. The loss was felt throughout the community of drivers

50

in Iraq. One driver who had heard of these killings, a deacon at a Baptist church in Sealy, Texas, hit a land mine the week before and was sure that God had protected him. They all count on the marines and soldiers with them, because no civilian truckers are allowed to carry weapons.

One thing these truckers are is patriotic. One of the drivers had been a Navy sailor on small boat crews on the rivers of Vietnam. He said that he had carried supplies in Vietnam to marines upriver, and now he carries supplies to marines up the road. He has already been in Iraq for two years. When I asked him how much longer he would be in Iraq, his reply took no thought: "I'll be here as long as the marines need me." All of these civilian drivers are proud to serve. They are a vital part of bringing much-needed supplies to units throughout Iraq, and so we pray for them.

Prayer for Those Who Serve Beside Us

ALL GAVE SOME AND SOME GAVE ALL.
—*Billy Ray Cyrus, "Some Gave All"*[8]

Lord,
We pray for those who have eighteen wheels
on the ground in Iraq and Afghanistan.
We pray for those civilians who provide services
wherever active-duty military goes.
We pray for those who face the same IEDs and mortars even
though they don't wear the military uniform or carry a weapon.
We pray for those who keep our troops well supplied and
taken care of despite the dangers they face every day.
We pray for these patriots—young and old, men and women.
We pray for those who have sacrificed alongside the troops.
May their pathways be smooth and straight.
And may you bring them safely home each day.
Amen and amen.

Prayer for Prisoners of War

DUTY. HONOR. COUNTRY. THOSE THREE HALLOWED WORDS
REVERENTLY DICTATE WHAT YOU OUGHT TO BE, WHAT YOU CAN BE,
WHAT YOU WILL BE. THEY ARE YOUR RALLYING POINT
TO BUILD COURAGE WHEN COURAGE SEEMS TO FAIL,
TO REGAIN FAITH WHEN THERE SEEMS TO BE LITTLE CAUSE
FOR FAITH, TO CREATE HOPE WHEN HOPE BECOMES FORLORN.
—*General Douglas MacArthur*[9]

Almighty God,
We gather today to give thanks for all those who have shown
duty and honor while being held as prisoners of war.
May we thank them by serving our country
honorably around the globe.
We count ourselves fortunate to serve in the
same tradition, and we vow never to forget the sacrifices,
pain, and isolation that they have suffered.
When we see them—identified at parades, by car license tags,
and by military medals—let us be the first ones
to step forward to thank them for their courage.
Perhaps some of their courage, faith, and hope will rub off
on us, and we will be better people because of
their presence in our lives.
We commend to you, O God, each person
who has been held as a prisoner of war.
We offer this prayer in honor of those who know more
about freedom than we can ever imagine.
Amen.

Prayer for Those Missing in Action

WHEN THERE IS A VISIBLE ENEMY TO FIGHT
IN OPEN COMBAT . . . MANY SERVE, ALL APPLAUD,
AND THE TIDE OF PATRIOTISM RUNS HIGH.
BUT WHEN THERE IS A LONG, SLOW STRUGGLE
WITH NO IMMEDIATE VISIBLE FOE,
YOUR CHOICE WILL SEEM HARD INDEED.
—*John F. Kennedy* [10]

Lord of All Who Serve . . .
Some of my brothers and sisters are missing . . .
In the forests of France . . .
The shallows of the South Pacific . . .
Mountains of Korea . . .
Jungles of Vietnam . . .
Sands of Iraq . . .
Parents grieving . . .
Marriages suspended . . .
Children without a parent . . .
We will search tirelessly . . .
We will pray unceasingly . . .
Until we are reunited . . .
Until we know . . .
And should they never return, may you keep them in heaven
until our reunion there.
Amen.

PAYING THE ULTIMATE PRICE

DOG TAGS

MCLAUGHLIN
P.J. A POS
000 00 0000
USN M
LUTHERAN

Someone hollers out across the emergency room tent: "Did anyone check his dog tags?"

Name, blood type, Social Security number, branch of service, sex, and religious preference.

It is the vital information that dangles from the chain around my neck and is laced into the laces of my left boot. I am no different from thousands of other service members in Iraq.

These five lines, imprinted in metal, can encapsulate the life of a military member. When a soldier is wounded and unable to speak, the dog tags are used to fill out the CTR (casualty treatment record). When a soldier is killed in action and lying on a stretcher, dog tags provide tentative identification. In those few crucial moments, a person's entire life is contained in five lines.

Name, blood type, Social Security number, branch of service, sex, and religious preference.

Dog tags.

Someone hollers out, "Check the dog tags!"

Prayer for Those Waiting on a Loved One

NEVER LET ME FORGET THAT
IT IS FAR BETTER TO LIGHT ONE CANDLE
THAN TO CURSE THE DARKNESS, AND TO JOIN MY LIGHT,
ONE DAY, WITH YOURS.
AMEN.
—*Prayer of St. Christopher*

Gracious God,
We join hearts with those who wait on a loved one.
Candles are lit in cathedrals;
Yellow ribbons are tied on trees, posts, and car antennas;
Flags are flown.
Be with husbands and wives, parents and grandparents,
children and friends.
Comfort those who worry and cry.
We will light candles together.
Family. Friends. Americans.
Amen.

Prayer for Those Paying the Greatest Price

SHARED JOY IS DOUBLE JOY
AND SHARED SORROW IS HALF SORROW.
—Swedish proverb

Gracious and Loving God,
This week many loved ones will turn
to you in worship and prayer.
Be with those families that have paid the greatest price.
Be with those who have lost a loved one.
Encircle them in your loving arms.
May they know that millions of Americans
are praying for them.
Together may their sorrows be halved as
we willingly carry this burden for them.
Fill us with compassion and grace.
In this mission of prayer we will never cease.
So be it and amen.

A MARINE ANGEL

Therefore encourage one another and build each other up
as you are already doing.
　—1 THESSALONIANS 5:11 HCSB

I work with angels, but not the type you might imagine.

The angels I'm talking about are American service members who are killed in action or killed by accidents in the combat zone. "Angel" is an actual designation used by the Marine Corps for the deceased.

I have done duty as the chaplain for the Mortuary Affairs unit at Camp Al Taqaddum, Iraq. I work with angels every week, sometimes every day, and too often many in one day. Fortunately, it has been fairly quiet lately.

Some of you may think that is a difficult job, and, yes, at times it is incredibly painful for the marines who do such a fine job at Mortuary Affairs. But many times it is a great honor, because these brave angels have done what the Bible says: "Greater love hath no man than this, that a man lay down his life for his friends" (John 15:13).

I want to tell you about a very special angel who taught me a powerful lesson about living. I know it may seem a little odd that a person killed in action would teach us about living, but this is a true and important story that all of you need to hear. It is a story about a marine.

A few days ago, a young man gave his life for his country and, more important, for the cause of freedom in Iraq. As is the case for many angels who arrive in Mortuary Affairs, this young man's story was told by his injury and the personal effects he carried.

While on patrol, this nineteen-year-old marine lance corporal was shot and mortally wounded by a sniper. The round that did the damage was found in the shoulder strap of his vest.

The doctors tried valiantly to save this marine. In a radical procedure called—in layman's terms—a clamshell thoracotomy, the surgeons opened his chest horizontally. It was a radical effort to stem the bleeding . . . to no avail.

So here you have three crucial elements in the story of our marine angel:

(1) He was a marine.
(2) At the age of nineteen, he was a lance corporal.
(3) He died in combat.

But this is just the beginning of what this marine's example teaches us.

He was proud of his Corps. On his left shoulder was a beautifully done tattoo of the eagle, globe, and anchor.

He was also a proud member of another group. On his right shoulder was a tattoo of a large Celtic cross, and his dog tags confirmed his Christian faith.

His personal effects filled out the rest of the story.

He had his hunting license—always a plus in the Corps. (If you took all the hunters out of the Corps, there wouldn't be many marines left.)

He also had something that speaks volumes about his character. Among the usual personal effects of driver's license, bank card, ID card, money, and the like, was scouting information that identified him as an Eagle Scout.

Still another card identified him as a Red Cross blood donor.

What are you seeing about this young man?

Around his neck with his dog tags was a pendant. Actually, half a pendant—the kind where you keep half and give the other half to a significant other.

So let's tally this up.

(1) A proud marine
(2) A nineteen-year-old lance corporal
(3) Died in combat fighting on behalf of his country and for Iraq's freedom
(4) A Christian (which should go first on the list!)
(5) A hunter (remember, always a bonus in the Marine Corps)
(6) An Eagle Scout
(7) A blood donor

Talk about using the talents that God had given him! And if seven is not enough, the last clue as to who he was came as quite a shock. While inventorying his equipment, one of the Mortuary Affair marines stopped when he found what appeared to be a picture in the band of the webbing inside his Kevlar helmet. As the marine opened the folded photo, I could see what it was. I knew from across the room what he held in his hand.

The room grew quiet as others saw what I saw . . .

It was a sonogram.

You could hear a pin drop.

You could hear hearts sink.

Typed on the sonogram were the words "Say hi to Mom and Grandma."

Add that to the tally of seven blessed traits an eighth: father-to-be.

I would have been honored to be this marine's chaplain. Wouldn't you want that type of person in your unit? We would hope for such a fine son.

His lesson to us is clear: Use all of the talents God has given you to the best of your abilities. None of us know the day or time of our death. Live a glorious life in service to God and others. Live a life for Christ. Live a life for your Corps, Navy, Army, or Air Force. Live life to the fullest.

Live a life in honor of this young marine who gave all. He will now be one of God's Marines and an inspiration to another in need.

Live a life in honor of those who have proudly and heroically worn a military uniform. We wear more than mere work clothes. Our uniforms represent history and tradition.

Live a life in honor of the One who gives you all you have and who gave his only Son so that you might live.

I urge you to dive in and live life like a young marine lance corporal—valiantly and heroically!

I was asked at my Fleet Marine Force officer qualification board what esprit de corps is. I know the answer now: it is the story of this young man and those who work with great respect to return him to his family.

I will carry this story with me proudly, and when someone asks me what it is like to serve in the military, I will tell the story of a young man who, in nineteen years, lived a life fuller than many of those twice his age. To do any less would dishonor God, who has given us so many incredible talents. To do any less would dishonor those who have sacrificed so much so that we might follow in their footsteps.

Live for God. Live for others. Live to your fullest.
There is a marine angel watching over you.
So be it. Amen.

Prayer for Those Who Grieve

I MUST BE STRONG AND CARRY ON
'CAUSE I KNOW I DON'T BELONG HERE IN HEAVEN.
—*Eric Clapton, "Tears in Heaven"*[11]

Lord,
Be with us in our times of grief—we know it is
the price of love—we will pay this price.
Our grief is a part of who we are—we know it will
change us forever—we can change.
Let us embrace our grief—we know it is
uniquely our own—we share it, but it is still our own.
Grief has turned to tears—tears have turned to music—
music touches our soul.
Our souls have been touched—we know that we are alive—
it is good to be alive even in pain.
Be with us in our times of grief—we know it is
the price of love—we will pay this price.
Amen.

A Prayer When Words Fail

I FEEL HOW WEAK AND FRUITLESS MUST BE
ANY WORDS OF MINE WHICH SHOULD ATTEMPT TO
BEGUILE YOU FROM GRIEF OF A LOSS SO OVERWHELMING.
—*Abraham Lincoln, in a letter to Mrs. Bixby,*
who lost five sons in the Civil War

God of Grace and Love,
Hear our prayer when we are at a loss for words.
Is "Thank you" enough for a veteran who lost a leg?
Is "I'm so sorry" enough for a young widow
whose husband was killed in action?
Is "If you need anything, call" enough for a
young sailor on a ship so far from home?
Hear our prayer when we are at a loss for words.
A casserole, a dessert, or a loaf of homemade bread with a note;
A hug, a kiss, or tears shed together.
We share our love when words fail.
Hear our prayer when we are at a loss for words.
Amen.

A SIDE OF THE STORY YOU WON'T SEE

I wish my fellow Americans were able to see the full picture of what is happening in Iraq. It is a sad commentary—and perhaps even quite unprofessional—that too many news outlets confuse the news and the editorial pages.

This has been one of the most difficult weeks in the nine months I've spent in Iraq, yet I heard from family and friends back in the States that most of the news this week was about Anna Nicole Smith and Britney Spears. That is my silver lining to the past week: I missed all the court battles and shaved-head stories.

This week American service members were living history here. For a brief moment this past Saturday (February 24, 2007), the lead story on CNN.com was about a truck bomber in the Al Anbar Province town of Habinayah, which is literally across a four-lane highway from us here at Camp Al Taqaddum (TQ). The resulting blast caused more than three dozen deaths, and I can personally attest to the medical treatment required of the nearly sixty wounded. These Iraqis were leaving worship—one of our most cherished rights in America. Families leaving worship were blown up—a devastating event when you see it in person—a sight that would change many minds of people at home who are ambivalent about this war.

Those sixty wounded received the best medical care available from every available surgeon, doctor, nurse, and corpsman at TQ. Even after a crash or blast, hospitals in the States wouldn't take that many people all at once. But the news media were not there to cover the hundreds of marines, sailors, soldiers, and airmen who lined up for hours to give blood in the "walking blood bank," knowing that they were giving blood to save Iraqis.

The news reporters missed the sorrow and consternation of the families who, coming out of worship at a mosque, had been targeted because their imam spoke out against the violence in his community. The story of local people speaking out against the insurgency does not sell copy or further fuel a press that seems increasingly antiwar. Can you imagine how the media would cover the story of people in the States coming out of church if they were bombed in such a savage manner just because they were exercising their rights to worship and speak openly?

I certainly wish the press would champion that cause of freedom here in Iraq. To live free is increasingly the cause of the people in Iraq, and that fact seems to be ignored by the press. Isn't it even New Hampshire's motto—"Live Free or Die?"

The reporters missed the thanks, waves, and hugs of these victims as they left the surgical unit to be escorted home. In many cases their torn and bloodied clothing had been replaced by sweat suits and flip-flops donated by regular, caring Americans back home. You see, a reporter staying in a hotel in Baghdad for a few days or even several weeks misses the whole picture. And, in turn, all of you back home miss the reason behind many of these senseless and cruel bombings as well as the incredible response of both the Iraqis and the Americans.

This is my second "big" mass casualty experience. On January 6, 2006, a suicide bomber detonated himself in line at a police recruitment effort in front of the glass factory in Ramadi. The bomber was sent there because of the overwhelming success of this recruitment effort. Our medical units throughout the region responded that day. The news, however, didn't report that within hours of the scene being secured and the wounded treated, more recruits lined up! In initial elections, less than 1 percent of the eligible Ramadi population voted. I was in Iraq in December 2005 for the general elections when 70 percent of those eligible in Ramadi voted. We don't turn out in those numbers at home—ever!

I will not deny that Iraq is still a very dangerous place and that there is a long journey ahead, but we are seeing more and more extraordinarily brave Iraqis. More and more people are voting, joining the army and the police force, and speaking out. The anti-Iraqi forces have increasingly resorted to inhumane bombings against their own people because of the progress being made. The bombings make the news, but not always the real reason behind them.

I have witnessed the lives of Iraqis saved by talented medical people who refused to be overwhelmed by such a mass casualty. I will never forget the look in the eyes of a marine staff sergeant as he held the hand of a little Iraqi boy who was seriously injured and separated from his family. The staff sergeant knew this boy was in dire straits. These two did not speak the same language. One was a Christian; the other, a Muslim. None of that mattered. They were two of God's children brought together by a senseless tragedy. It was a moment that will forever affect the life of that marine. They did not separate hands until the litter bearers swept the boy away to a waiting helicopter.

I am extremely proud of this marine and honored to share his Marine Corps heritage by wearing the same uniform. You won't see that compassionate story in the news . . . I just thought you ought to know.

Prayer for God's Constant Presence

O GOD, OUR HELP IN AGES PAST,
OUR HOPE FOR YEARS TO COME . . .
—*Isaac Watts, "O God, Our Help in Ages Past"*

Ever-Present God,
O God, our help in ages past,
On bended knee we seek your grace.
We search for answers in this holy place,
Head bowed and eyes closed tight,
Seeking you with all our might.
O God, our help in ages past,
Our shelter from the stormy blast,
Prayers to your Holy Place we cast:
Be with us now and ever more.
In grateful love our hearts do soar.
We know where safety lies
And where hope is from.
You are our shield this hour
And for all the times to come.
O God, our help in ages past,
Our Eternal Home.
Amen.

THE ARMED FORCES FAMILY

Prayer of Indebtedness

MY FATHER DIDN'T TELL ME HOW TO LIVE;
HE LIVED, AND LET ME WATCH HIM DO IT.
—*Clarence Budington Kelland*

God of All Generations,
Debts are remembered today.
We have not arrived here by ourselves.
We are indebted to countless generations.
We are indebted to those who have found cures for diseases.
We are indebted to those who have established free societies.
We are indebted to those who have kept societies free.
We are indebted to those who have led faith-filled lives.
We are indebted to those who have taught in schools.
We are indebted to those who have supported families.
We are indebted to those whose names we do not know.
Debts are remembered today.
We have not arrived here by ourselves.
Amen.

A TRADITION OF SERVICE

I sent an e-mail to my father asking about the history of military service in our family. I knew that he had shipped overseas to the South Pacific as a surveyor in the Army just as the armistice was signed ending the Korean War. And from childhood I recalled memories of my granddad (my father's father) going to the American Legion Post several nights a week. Upon receiving my father's e-mail reply, I was astonished and proud of my family's military service record.

All four uncles on my mother's side of the family saw active-duty service. Three served in the Army and one in the Air Force. Three of my four uncles on my father's side of the family also served, two in the Army and one in the Air Force. Uncle Carl and Uncle Charles both saw combat in Korea.

My father closed his e-mail by saying this: "At least seven out of your eight uncles served their country. Now it's your turn—and your children's—to carry on the proud tradition."

All of us are indebted to the generations of men and women who have secured our freedom by their quiet willingness to serve in the armed forces of the United States. My father and my uncles, like so many of their contemporaries, grew up believing this was their duty. Call it a part of basic American citizenship. Serving God and country was foundational to the values of many young Americans in the 1940s and '50s. Before them, many of their fathers had served in either World War I or World War II.

Now I take my place, hoping and praying to be courageous enough to

74

uphold the proud tradition of the millions who have served in our military. We are indebted, and we offer a prayer of thanks for all who have served. We offer our prayers in memory of the heroic men and women in uniform who have given the ultimate sacrifice of their lives for our freedom.

Prayer for Those Called to Serve

When he shall die,
Take him and cut him out in little stars,
And he will make the face of heaven so fine
That all the world will be in love with night
And pay no worship to the garish sun.
—*Juliet in William Shakespeare's* Romeo and Juliet

Gracious God,
We humbly ask your help that we, too, may live a life that
would illuminate the heavens when our days on this earth end.
We humbly ask your help that we may live this life here
and now bringing goodwill, good words,
and good actions before our days on this earth end.
There is no greater calling than to love
and serve you and our fellow man.
Let us live with grace today.
Amen.

FREEDOM OF THE WILL

I will die for my faith.

I will die for my country.

I will die for those I serve with.

I will die for my wife and children.

It is my choice: I do not pick or know my appointed time or place of death, but I willingly choose to serve in dangerous places.

It is my choice: I place my God, my country, and my family before myself. It is a choice that I have in common with hundreds of thousands of my military brothers and sisters. It is the freedom of the will.

Make no mistake. The US military member wants to serve with honor and distinction and then safely return home. We are willing to serve for freedom, and we do so for those who do not believe exactly as we do in order to protect their right to believe as they wish.

Pray for those who are willing to guarantee all of us the right to pray, worship, believe, and live as we choose. Pray that we may continue to freely choose to serve—and serve wholeheartedly.

Prayer for a Marine

AND WHEN HE GOES TO HEAVEN
TO SAINT PETER HE WILL TELL:
ANOTHER MARINE REPORTING, SIR;
I'VE SERVED MY TIME IN HELL!
—*Epitaph of Private First Class Cameron, USMC, Guadalcanal, 1942*

Lord,
Marines guard us by day and night, standing tall and true;
A picture of freedom with a blood stripe
of red on a trouser of blue.
Grant that we give each one dignity, respect, and our thanks;
We would be proud if one of our children
were to join in their ranks.
Bless each marine who remains always faithful.
For the peace they provide, we'll always be grateful.
Keep them safe from harm on every distant shore.
We pray that peace comes, and we'll need them no more.
But should there be a call for liberty, a whimper, or a cry,
We know they'll be there—do or die. Semper Fi.
Amen, Marine. Amen.

RED BULL, GATORADE, AND MARLBOROS

Pray for three things for our troops on convoys: Red Bull, Gatorade, and Marlboros. That's right. And pray for the companies that own and produce Red Bull energy drink, Gatorade, and Marlboros! Pray that they can keep up with the demand for these products that keep our troops happy.

Marines, especially young ones, live on Red Bull. They often work eighteen- to twenty-hour days, seven days a week, seven to twelve months straight, and they need the caffeine to stay awake. Kids—and I call them kids because I am easily old enough to be their father—don't drink too much coffee. But when you operate for thirty-six to forty-eight hours straight with no sleep in a combat environment, you have to stay awake. Red Bull is the drink of choice to keep the troops on their toes. And you haven't lived till you've had Red Bull on ice served in a plastic water bottle that's been cut in half.

In addition to these long hours, another constant in Iraq is the hot and dry desert. Everyone gets tired of water. Like it or not, you have to push a lot of fluids through your system just to stay even and avoid dehydration. So Gatorade is consumed by the caseload. Yes, Gatorade has the needed electrolytes to replenish the system, but mostly it has some flavor. Premade or in powdered form, Gatorade is the thirst quencher of choice not just for athletes but for marines fighting in the scorching desert temperatures reaching 130 degrees.

The final constant is a practice common to each war in the history of the United States: troops in the field smoke much more than they do at home. Perhaps it soothes the nerves while they wait to go into harm's way.

Maybe it makes little difference that smoking is bad for your health. So are bullets, land mines, and IEDs!

At four thirty in the morning, it is amazing to see the strong constitution of our young marines. Red Bull, Gatorade, and Marlboros make for quite a sight. Oh, to be eighteen years old, fearless, and in possession of a cast-iron stomach!

And if you will, pray for a fourth thing: the safety of these incredible young men and women.

THE LOOK OF A CONVOY

A skeleton key tied to a belt, a tiny ceramic angel in the top right pocket, a footprints-of-Jesus pin under the flap of the top left pocket, a New Testament from Mom in the top left pocket, a rosary from Grandmother, and now a crucifix from the chaplain. These are the trinkets—the protectors, if you will—for one marine lance corporal headed out on a convoy.

A lucky wrench on a flak jacket . . . an ace of spades on a helmet . . . photos of girlfriend, wife, kids . . . all types of crosses and rosaries . . . a laminated four-leaf clover . . . a lucky T-shirt . . . medals of St. Mary, St. Christopher, and St. Michael the Archangel (patron saint of marines) . . . even a medal of St. Jude, the patron saint of hopeless causes . . . All these trinkets, religious medallions, and many more items—too many to list—are quietly carried by this platoon of very young marines. As a chaplain, I, too, am a good-luck charm. It is bad luck not to say a prayer before leaving. Requesting the protection of the Almighty has a place in each convoy briefing, as does the checking of equipment and the description of the route and its threats.

After only a month in Iraq, "in country," these young men and women have a rougher edge. They are a bit dirty and have already begun aging two months for every month they are in country. They can fall asleep in a matter of moments on a concrete slab or draped across the hood of a Humvee in wicked heat while wearing full battle gear.

I would follow them anywhere and, as a noncombatant, entrust my life to their care. And they entrust their lives to a first lieutenant barely older than many of them. America entrusts its freedom to soldiers like these who serve in our armed forces.

To me, this gathering for a convoy is a magnificent sight, and I am honored to speak to them, read Scripture, pray, and leave them with a special blessing.

Blessing for a Convoy

May the Lord bless you and keep you.
May the road be smooth and straight.
May your Humvees and trucks run strong and true.
May your wreckers and tow trucks remain empty.
May the desert wind be cool at your back.
And may the Lord bring you safely home.
In the name of the Father, and of the Son,
and of the Holy Spirit.
Amen.

Prayer for a Sailor

THEY THAT GO DOWN TO THE SEA IN SHIPS,
THAT DO BUSINESS IN GREAT WATERS;
THESE SEE THE WORKS OF THE LORD,
AND HIS WONDERS IN THE DEEP.
—*Psalm 107:23–24*

Eternal Father,
Aboard frigates and carriers and vessels of all types,
we come to you
To ask protection for sailors on the oceans blue.
The ocean is so big, and each ship so small;
Only you can keep watch over them all.
For freedom's sake they've been known to boast
That sailors can bring protection to any coast.
Still, from seaman to admiral, our prayer is the same:
That the world might know peace in your Holy Name.
Amen, Sailor. Amen.

NAVY TRADITION

- *Sailors wear crackerjacks.*
- *Four bells ring when the ship's captain boards or departs from the vessel.*
- *The ship's company observes ritual ceremonies when crossing the equator.*
- *Chief petty officers throw mugs overboard when crossing over the Mariana Trench.*
- *New petty officers "tack on the crow" when they are promoted to third class.*

The Navy, like the other branches of military, is steeped in traditions. Some of these traditions are as serious as the ceremony marking the transfer of command, and some are as inane as gathering new crew members on the deck to observe the fictional "International Date Line Buoy Field", a ruse to fool gullible shipmates and break up the monotony of long days at sea.

Prayer has its place in Navy tradition. Specifically, when the ship is at sea, tradition dictates that an evening prayer is said five minutes before the playing of taps. If the ship's company includes a chaplain, he or she will offer the prayer over the ship's intercom. Evening prayer dates back to a time when sailors were without the modern conveniences of radio and radar and found themselves at the mercy of the seas. And so, as long as the seas and the missions remain dangerous, evening prayer for the crew will be officially and unofficially observed on United States naval vessels.

When sailing through rough seas and dangerous waters, all the while separated from family and friends, sailors find immeasurable comfort in hearing a prayer for safety, continued protection, or watch over loved ones. Sailors do not have the reputation of being the world's most religious group of individuals, but they may be among the most God-fearing and God-respecting groups. After all, sailors know that the ocean is great and their ship is small.

Among my collection of memorabilia from my three years as the chaplain on board the USS *Princeton* (CG-59) is a journal with a worn-out cover that contains each of the evening prayers I offered during my two six-month deployments and numerous other operations at sea. The journal reminds me of God's presence and the comfort he gave the crew. Some of the prayers are serious in nature, and others are humorous. Every prayer began with an inspirational quote for those in the crew who might hear a quote more easily than a prayer. Each prayer was meant to encourage the crew and remind them of our dependence on God and one another. Here is the quote and evening prayer I gave onboard the *Princeton* on November 1, 1993, while we were deployed in the Persian Gulf:

"There is no limit to what can be accomplished if it doesn't matter who gets the credit." —Ralph Waldo Emerson

Let us pray: Lord, I give thanks tonight for all in our crew who have given unselfishly of their own time and effort to keep us all safe and make us successful. Help each of us to give credit where it is due. To date, we have accomplished every task placed in front of us. Help us to continue in this spirit so that we may all return safely. We ask this prayer and all others in your holy name. Amen.

Every night sailors pray at sea, and their families pray ashore. Calling on God in times of need is a tradition well worth keeping. And so we pray:

Eternal Father, strong to save,
Whose arm has bound the restless wave . . .
O hear us when we cry to thee
For those in peril on the sea!

Prayer for a Soldier

I DIDN'T RAISE MY BOY TO BE A SOLDIER.
—*Alfred Bryan, "A Mother's Plea for Peace" (1915)*

Almighty God,
Green camouflage uniforms stretch row upon row,
Men proud to serve wherever they are told to go.
Keep every soldier under your care,
For courage like theirs is extremely rare.
Whether serving in the air, on the ground, or inside of tanks,
Let them know our country owes them resounding thanks.
And if the conflicts of the world will not cease,
Be with the soldiers who will bring us peace.
Amen, Soldier. Amen.

PRAYING WITH AN INJURED SOLDIER

It is a Saturday, and the soldiers at the combat outpost near Ramadi are taking a pounding from the insurgents' mortar rounds.

The operating room stays busy for twelve straight hours. The medical team does an exceptional job. Soldiers with serious injuries are stabilized. At the end of the day, which has now almost rolled into Sunday, we are grateful that none of the soldiers here or at the combat outpost have lost their lives.

I have the honor of meeting five soldiers who will receive the Purple Heart.

In the midst of the hectic activity, I take a few moments to speak with these fine young men. I find out where they are from, reassure them that they are receiving outstanding medical care, tell them that we're all proud of their bravery, offer to pray with them now, and promise to pray for them after they leave.

Without exception, each soldier welcomes the prayers and is put a little more at ease during this otherwise frightening day.

So, for a sergeant and a private first class from Pennsylvania, a sergeant first class from Michigan, a sergeant from Ohio, and a corporal from Virginia—who are heroes and Purple Heart recipients—I offer this prayer:

Almighty God,
I pray now with this soldier.
All of us working here thank him for his service, his bravery,
    and his efforts that keep us safe.
Be with him now.
Guide his doctors, nurses, and corpsmen.

Ease his worries and those of his family and friends.
Bind up his wounds and make him whole.
Return him home safely.
We pray in your holy name.
Amen.

I find out that three of the five soldiers are from the same unit, and they ask me to pray for their unit. They are scheduled to leave Iraq in less than two months after spending more than ten months in country. Remarkably, each one of them has asked the same question totally independent of one another: "Can I recover in Kuwait or Germany and go home with my unit?"

I have to tell them no and explain that they'll be home in another week or two. Each of them understands, yet each of them has tears rolling quietly down his cheeks as he lies on his stretcher. Such is their loyalty and devotion to their unit.

I say a silent prayer of thanksgiving for these soldiers and for all the soldiers of the combat outpost who face tremendous danger each day.

May God be with them.

Prayer for an Airman

NEVER IN THE FIELD OF HUMAN CONFLICT
WAS SO MUCH OWED BY SO MANY TO SO FEW.
—*Winston Churchill, on British airmen*
in anticipation of the Battle of Britain

Lord of the Skies and Heaven,
They are the ones who patrol the wild blue yonder.
In the fight to secure freedom, you'll find none fonder.
From the skies high above, out of plain sight,
They proudly protect our nation by day and by night.
Whether they're soaring like birds,
turning wrenches, or securing supplies,
O Lord, you are where the airmen's true protection lies.
We pray for the Air Force on bended knee
As they soar high above, closer to thee.
Amen, Airman. Amen.

Prayer for a Coastguardsman

THE PRICE OF FREEDOM IS ETERNAL VIGILANCE.
—*Thomas Jefferson*

SEMPER PARATUS
—*"Always ready," the motto of the US Coast Guard*

God of All Glory,
We pray for the men and women
who guard both river and coast.
They stand always ready where we need them most.
Risking their lives through flood or gale,
The Coast Guard is ready to answer the mariner's hail.
Drugs or terror, they answer the call.
Coast Guard service—among the bravest of all.
Be with the Coast Guard, we ask and we pray,
As they protect in quiet our waters each day.
Amen, Coastie. Amen.

COASTIES

Most people, even other military people, know very little about the United States Coast Guard. My friends were surprised to find out that I am a Coast Guard chaplain. I have to explain to them, "No, it's not like the Civil Air Patrol," and "Yes, I am still an active-duty Navy chaplain."

The questions continue: "But isn't the Coast Guard in the Department of Transportation?"

"Used to be." I explain further, "But now they're a part of the Department of Homeland Security."

Still confused, they ask me, "Did you do a lateral transfer to the Coast Guard?"

The fact is that active-duty Navy chaplains serve as chaplains to the Coast Guard. We receive orders to their units, and we wear their uniforms the same as we receive orders to Marine Corps units and wear Marine Corps uniforms.

I served with "Coasties" on my third tour, just after a tour with the Marine Corps. I found out that the Coast Guard is just as professional, dedicated, and motivated as the Marine Corps. Don't let the blue uniforms and longer hair fool you. Coasties don't train as much simply because they are doing their job each day. Whether it is patrolling and marking rivers or coastal waters, doing Arctic icebreaker patrols, interdicting drug traffic, patrolling fisheries, stopping illegal immigration, or saving the lives of boaters, members of the Coast Guard do their job each day instead of training for a future mission. People are also surprised to find Coasties training our Navy as well as other allied navies around the world in doing port security and boardings and inspections in the Persian Gulf.

If you have questions about the Coast Guard, just talk to a commercial fisherman in the Bering Strait who has been rescued in some of the worst weather imaginable. Coasties will fly helicopters and planes and drive ships into weather conditions that often make other military pilots and Navy ship captains shake their heads in disbelief.

When you pray for Coasties, know that they go into harm's way each and every day to keep our nation safe. Know, too, that embedded in their units are Navy chaplains who are proud to wear the Coast Guard uniform.

If I am fortunate enough to get orders back to a Coast Guard unit, I will proudly wear its blue colors and pray for their safety each day.

Prayer for the National Guard and Reserves

THERE IS A TIME TO PRAY AND A TIME TO FIGHT,
AND THAT TIME HAS NOW COME.
—*Rev. Peter Muhlenberg in a sermon at Woodstock, Virginia, 1775.*
After the sermon, the Reverend Muhlenberg took off
his clerical robes to reveal his military uniform.

Merciful God,
From bankers to students and that's not all,
Americans leave jobs to answer the call.
Training on weekends while others rest.
Dedication and motivation none can contest.
Honor their sacrifice when they join the ranks.
Let us never forget to give them thanks.
Keep them safe at home or abroad.
Their undying commitment we stand to applaud.
Amen, Guard and Reserve. Amen.

THEY'RE NOT WEEKEND WARRIORS

In the year of our Lord 1314,
patriots of Scotland, starving and outnumbered,
charged the fields of Bannockburn.
They fought like warrior poets.
They fought like Scotsmen. And won their freedom.
—FROM THE MOVIE *BRAVEHEART*[12]

For centuries, everyday, ordinary citizens have left their families and jobs to answer the call of freedom. The war in Iraq is no exception. In fact, the Reserves and National Guard have taken on more than their fair share of the load in Iraq.

On August 28, 2005, I landed in Kuwait. Within hours I was flown via a C-130 to Camp Al Taqaddum, Iraq. The C-130 was piloted and crewed by the Michigan Air National Guard. This would begin my long association with the Guard and Reserve in Iraq.

California, Wyoming, Georgia, Montana, Ohio, Pennsylvania, Michigan, North Carolina, Arizona, South Carolina, Alabama, Virginia, Texas, Illinois, Kansas, Kentucky, Massachusetts, Maine, Minnesota, Nebraska, Tennessee, Washington, Rhode Island, and Idaho come to mind when I remember patients in Surgical Shock Trauma and angels from Mortuary Affairs. I know that I have forgotten some of the states of the reservists and guardsmen I have met, but I will never forget their heroism or their stories.

I saw a first lieutenant from the Michigan National Guard in the SSTP three times! He was known to the crew as "the guy who shot an insurgent through a cow"—and I'll explain. On his second appearance in the SSTP, to have fragments removed from his right leg, the first lieutenant told us how they had cornered twenty insurgents in a house. One of the enemy decided to fire a rocket-propelled grenade (RPG) and then make a break for it. The RPG wounded the first lieutenant, and it also made him mad. The insurgent got no farther than trying to hide in a field behind a cow. Not knowing if the insurgent had another grenade to load in his tube, the lieutenant fired a round that went right through the cow and killed the insurgent. On his third visit to the SSTP a month later, the lieutenant had fragmentation in his left leg that required surgery and his being sent back to the United States. Interestingly enough, his civilian job was making the up-armor packages for equipment in Iraq.

Sooner or later it seems like you've seen it all. We had brothers from the Pennsylvania National Guard arrive at the SSTP a week apart. One had severely injured his hand with a .50 caliber round. The other had been at his post near Ramadi when he saw an insurgent through his binoculars just as the insurgent shot at him, wounding him in the forearm. I can't begin to imagine his parents' surprise and shock when they received the second phone call about their second son. They thought the call was an update on the first son's injury. Instead, his mother fainted when told that her other son had been shot.

As tough as it must have been on those parents, I won't forget another family, also of the Pennsylvania National Guard. Not brothers, but father and sons! The father is a very good medic we're familiar with at the SSTP. We've seen him bringing in wounded troops from the field on several occasions. Nothing was harder for him, though, than the day he found out that one of those wounded troops was his son! It was a tearful yet joyful reunion because the son's wounds were not life threatening. A week later I saw this medic again and asked how his son was doing. Much to my surprise, the medic wanted to know which son. It turns out that he is in Iraq with two of his sons!

Many active-duty service members refer to the Guard and Reserves as "weekend warriors" since they drill once a month (usually from Friday to Sunday) and for a two-week stretch sometime during the year. "Weekend warriors" is generally a derogatory term that makes fun of the training that many of these men and women receive.

After spending time in Iraq, however, I've determined I will never use that term in jest. As the first lieutenant lay in the recovery room after surgery, he made a very wise observation: "I guess they can't call me a weekend warrior anymore."

This young man has a combat-action ribbon and multiple Purple Heart medals to his credit, so no one has the right to say he's merely a weekend warrior. I pray for these men and women, these citizen soldiers who follow in the centuries-old tradition of putting aside their suits and work clothes to proudly wear a military uniform and fight alongside their active-duty counterparts. They're definitely not weekend warriors.

Prayer for a Fallen Marine

IF I AM INCLINED TO DOUBT, STEADY MY FAITH;
IF I AM TEMPTED, MAKE ME STRONG TO RESIST;
IF I SHOULD MISS THE MARK, GIVE ME COURAGE TO TRY AGAIN.
GUIDE ME WITH THE LIGHT OF TRUTH
AND GRANT ME WISDOM BY WHICH
I MAY UNDERSTAND THE ANSWER TO MY PRAYER.
AMEN.

—*The Marine's Prayer*

Merciful and Gracious God,
We call on you today to help us understand
why outstanding marines die so young.
We call on you today to heal our broken hearts.
We call on you today to bind us with
courage and strength to carry on in their place.
We call on you today to open your gracious arms
to accept one of your own.
We call on you today to bestow on our
fallen brothers the great honor of being called
one of *God's* Marines.
We offer this prayer in memory of marines
who have paid the ultimate price.
Once a marine, always and eternally a marine.
Ooo-rah and amen.

98

WHERE ANGELS TREAD

Let brotherly love continue.
Be not forgetful to entertain strangers:
for thereby some have entertained angels unawares.
—HEBREWS 13:1–2

Halfway through my deployment to Iraq, I am given an added assignment. In addition to my duties as chaplain to the Surgical Shock Trauma Platoon, I am assigned to be chaplain to the marines who take care of angels, of those who have died here in Iraq. The marines of Mortuary Affairs (MA) have what is termed "no tougher duty, no greater honor."

Angels can be American military or civilians, Iraqi Security Forces or civilians, third-country nationals working in Iraq, and even enemy combatants. Without exception, the marines who recover and prepare the deceased for shipment back to the States, return to relatives in Iraq, return to their country of origin, or burial in accordance with Muslim customs are professionals of the highest caliber: they treat each angel with dignity and respect.

When the preparation of each angel is complete, the crew gathers around the flag-draped transfer case for the reading of Scripture and prayer. We stand together as family, and together we stand in for the unit of the deceased. We do not know if the angel has brothers or sisters, but we stand in for family as well. We stand together with great pride, dignity, and sorrow. We stand together for each angel, and we pray for grace, mercy, and forgiveness regardless of nationality, creed, or religion, because we share a common bond as the children of God. We acknowledge that we are trying to live in accordance with God's will but that we sometimes fall short—as evidenced by this war. It is a solemn moment for all involved. It reminds us of the shortness and fragility of our own lives.

These MA marines are often called on to go the extra mile to locate and recover angels still on the battlefield. In these instances, they put themselves at great personal risk, and some of the crew have the scars and Purple Hearts to prove it. It would be fair to say that the crew never fully gets used to this difficult task. Each angel who passes through Mortuary Affairs takes a little bit out of the individual crew members. As their chaplain, I would worry more about them if they were not affected by the ravages of war and death.

I know the crew of Mortuary Affairs entertains angels. When my career in the Navy is over, I will probably have no prouder moments than those in which I was privileged to honor the fallen heroes in Iraq. Pray for those who do the most difficult of jobs in our military.

A Warrior's Prayer for Peace

EVERY GUN THAT IS MADE, EVERY WARSHIP LAUNCHED,
EVERY ROCKET FIRED SIGNIFIES, IN THE FINAL SENSE, A THEFT
FROM THOSE WHO HUNGER AND ARE NOT FED,
THOSE WHO ARE COLD AND ARE NOT CLOTHED.
THIS WORLD IN ARMS IS NOT SPENDING MONEY ALONE.
IT IS SPENDING THE SWEAT OF ITS LABORERS,
THE GENIUS OF ITS SCIENTISTS, THE HOPE OF ITS CHILDREN.
THIS IS NOT A WAY OF LIFE AT ALL IN ANY TRUE SENSE.
UNDER THE CLOUDS OF WAR,
IT IS HUMANITY HANGING FROM A CROSS OF IRON.
—*Dwight D. Eisenhower* [13]

Mighty God,
Be merciful and hear the prayers of all warriors today.
We pray for peace in this land and around the world.
As warriors, we know that our brothers and sisters
will pay the highest costs of war if there is no peace.
Be merciful and hear the prayers of all warriors today.
We pray for a quick and lasting end to this war.
As Americans, we know that the money being spent here
can be used in other ways.
Be merciful and hear the prayers of all warriors today.
We pray knowing that you have told us,
"Blessed are the peacemakers."
As humanity, we have been unable to attain peace on earth.
Be merciful and hear the prayers of all warriors today.
We pray on bended knees.
We pray with wounded hearts.
Be merciful and hear the prayers of all warriors today.
Amen and amen.

THE CURRENT AND FUTURE RESULTS OF THE ARMS RACE

You reap what you sow . . .

Sow the wind; reap the whirlwind . . .

I always wonder when the insurgency, enemy, warring factions, anti-Iraqi forces, whatever they are called this week—I wonder when they will run out of ammunition, mortars, rockets, bombs, and on and on and on.

Perhaps everyone who owns stock in a defense industry company should think long and hard about that. Some weapons being used against American forces were sold to Iraq by America and its allies decades ago. The amount of munitions the enemy expends in just one week here in Iraq is astounding. Then take into account the amount that US troops use each week, and the total amounts. Add in the amount coming over the borders from Iran and Syria. Toss in the Russian-made AK-47s, Chinese rockets, and a plethora of former Iron Curtain country armaments, and the amount becomes staggering.

The worldwide arms race of the 1950s, '60s, '70s, and '80s adds up to tonnages none of us can fathom even if we were able to put a ballpark figure on the total amount.

I wonder this because just this afternoon another rocket landed on this forward operating base.

The arms race, we were told, would keep us safe by means of deterrence. Did we forget that the rest of the world was racing at the same time? By all measures, the arms race, while not currently a front-burner concern of the world or the media, still exists.

From my point of view here in Iraq, all those old weapons that so many companies worldwide made money manufacturing are not a deterrent. They are, in fact, life-threatening.

They sow the wind and reap the whirlwind. (NIV)

Not my words, but rather those of the prophet Hosea in Hosea 8:7, a lesson he sought to teach Israel in 715 BC.

You reap what you sow.

Not my words, but those of the apostle Paul in Galatians. Here is what he said in full:

Do not be deceived: God cannot be mocked. A man reaps what he sows. The one who sows to please his sinful nature, from that nature will reap destruction; the one who sows to please the Spirit, from the Spirit will reap eternal life. Let us not become weary in doing good, for at the proper time we will reap a harvest if we do not give up. Therefore, as we have opportunity, let us do good to all people, especially to those who belong to the family of believers. (Galatians 6:7–10 NIV)

Hundreds upon hundreds of years ago, Hosea and Paul wrote these messages from God for all of us.

As one who is called to pray for peace in the middle of a war, I hope that we do not become weary of doing what is good and right.

I fear the reaping of the earthly results of the arms race, but not as much as I fear the heavenly result upon my own judgment day.

If you have the opportunity today, heed Paul's words to the churches in Galatia: do what is good, pray for peace, advocate for peace, and then be joyous because you have sown to please God and will reap the everlasting harvest found in his graciousness.

I wonder, *What if the enemy only runs out of munitions when we do?*

Prayer for Quiet Heroes

THEREFORE WHEN THOU DOEST THINE ALMS, DO NOT
SOUND A TRUMPET BEFORE THEE, AS THE HYPOCRITES DO
IN THE SYNAGOGUES AND IN THE STREETS, THAT THEY
MAY HAVE GLORY OF MEN. VERILY I SAY UNTO YOU,
THEY HAVE THEIR REWARD. BUT WHEN THOU DOEST ALMS,
LET NOT THY LEFT HAND KNOW WHAT THY RIGHT HAND DOETH.
—Matthew 6:2–3

Lord,
Every day there are heroes here who
never call attention to themselves.
Bless and protect them.
Every day people here do unto others
as they would have others do unto them.
Bless and protect them.
Every day people here love their neighbors as themselves.
Bless and protect them.
Every day people here live out the gospel of grace and hope.
Bless and protect them.
Strengthen us by their example,
for it speaks louder than any words ever can.
Amen.

THE WALKING BLOOD BANK

You will meet family members and friends who return from combat and never know that they are heroes. You will never know that they saved a life, and most likely, they won't tell you that they did even if they know. But I will tell you about them, because without these thousands of quiet heroes, Americans and Iraqis alike would lose their lives each day.

The call comes across the radio that someone is injured and in urgent need of surgery. Surgeons are called on to literally stem the tide of death. One of the greatest dangers to the critically wounded is the loss of blood. While surgeons and anesthesiologists fight to contain the loss of blood and then make sure blood pressures return to normal, they are assisted in their efforts by an unsung cast of service members.

Blood is in limited and all too often exhaustible supply at combat trauma centers. To ensure that enough blood is available to treat a critically injured patient, the call for blood goes out across the base at a moment's notice.

An e-mail goes out simply saying that the Walking Blood Bank is now open for whatever blood type is needed. When the message showing your blood type flashes up on your screen, you get up and walk, run, or even drive from wherever you are on base to donate blood. The reality is, if people don't respond to this call, there is a strong likelihood that the patient in surgery will be in grave danger.

In two tours of duty in Iraq, I have yet to see a Walking Blood Bank that didn't have more donors than needed.

The goodness of the spirit of American service members is demonstrated in this time of need. When they show up to donate blood, they have

105

no idea who is receiving their blood. Their blood could be used for a marine or soldier, a member of the Iraqi police or army, an Iraqi civilian, or even an enemy prisoner of war. It doesn't matter to the donors.

I've watched people stand in line for a couple of hours during a mass casualty situation in which multiple blood types were needed for Iraqi civilians.

When blood is no longer needed, that message goes out again to all computers. People who have waited in line are thanked and asked to show up the next time the Walking Blood Bank is open, since the people who donated today are not eligible to donate for another six weeks.

No one has ever received an award or a medal for donating blood to save another person's life. These soldiers expect nothing more than a handshake and the personal satisfaction that they have done their duty to humanity.

You are surrounded by heroes. Quiet heroes. So whenever you meet members of the armed forces, shake their hands and thank them. There is a good chance that they have saved a life. I know that they will be greatly rewarded in heaven.

Prayer for a Good Pair of Boots

I WILL ALWAYS OBEY YOUR LAW,
FOR EVER AND EVER.
I WILL WALK ABOUT IN FREEDOM,
FOR I HAVE SOUGHT OUT YOUR PRECEPTS.
—*Psalm 119:44–45 NIV*

Lord,
We're out here walkin' and kickin' up a lot of sand and dust,
Blazing a trail for others to walk
with the same freedom we have at home.
So if you could make sure all the soldiers, sailors, marines,
and airmen have a good pair of boots, I'd be grateful.
Some Bates, steel-toed, Vibram-soled,
hot-weather models would do nicely.
You see, Lord, a lot of your proud servants here in the desert
spend hours and even days on end wearing their boots.
Some socks and Odor-Eater insoles would be appreciated too.
We all know that you have some important prayers to hear,
but this one is pretty important to us as we sometimes
have to use our boots to get out of tight situations.
And we'd like some boots for our Iraqi counterparts so that
they will know what it feels like to walk in freedom's shoes too!
Thank you, Lord. (And one pair of size 12 for me.)
Your humble servant.
Amen.

WALKING AND TALKING TO GOD

When you come to Iraq, the most valuable piece of equipment you are issued is a good pair of boots. Boots are worn anywhere from twelve to twenty-four hours a day—and sometimes even longer. They are worn in sand, heat, rain, and mud. They have to be comfortable because you walk everywhere. I've seen all different types of boots—some used to get out of danger, some worn until the soles came apart, some that would knock the stink off a camel—all of them full of sand and covered with mud or dust.

However, all of this walking is a good thing, not so much for the physical workout, but rather for the spiritual exercise. It is appropriate that we spend a lot of time walking around and kicking up the sand and dust in a place where many Old Testament events took place.

For all of the violence and military presence, Iraq is still a place to walk and talk with God on a daily basis. It is even more appropriate on one US base in particular—the Al Asad air base that was built in 1985 by Saddam Hussein. Within the borders of the base is a place called Abraham's Oasis. It is believed to be the stopping point on Abraham's journey mentioned in Genesis 11.

Plenty of biblical characters spent time walking and talking to God in the desert. Jonah, for instance, had to cross modern-day Iraq to reach Nineveh.

Prayer and walking have seemed to go together throughout time. Some of our deepest conversations with God happen as we walk, whether we are traversing the desert, pacing the halls of a hospital, strolling the sidewalks

108

of our neighborhoods, meditating as we walk the sandy shoreline, or seeking solace and retreat on forest trails.

So get a sturdy, yet comfortable pair of boots, walk and talk, kick up some sand . . . God is always waiting and listening.

Prayer at an Enlistment/Reenlistment

I DO SOLEMNLY SWEAR (OR AFFIRM)
THAT I WILL SUPPORT AND DEFEND
THE CONSTITUTION OF THE UNITED STATES
AGAINST ALL ENEMIES, FOREIGN AND DOMESTIC;
THAT I WILL BEAR TRUE FAITH AND ALLEGIANCE TO THE SAME;
AND THAT I WILL OBEY THE ORDERS
OF THE PRESIDENT OF THE UNITED STATES
AND THE ORDERS OF THE OFFICERS APPOINTED OVER ME,
ACCORDING TO REGULATIONS AND
THE UNIFORM CODE OF MILITARY JUSTICE.
SO HELP ME GOD.

—Oath of Enlistment

God who Protects and Saves:
Grant me faithfulness to you, O God.
Grant me loyalty to the United States of America.
Grant me discipline in following orders.
Grant me allegiance to the men and women around me.
Grant me the courage to live up to the highest ideals.
Grant me the stamina to discharge my duties.

Amen.

110

THERE IS NO FINER SIGHT

Have you ever seen marines returning straight from the battlefield? Brown. Totally brown from the tops of their crew cuts to the well-worn soles of their combat boots. Covered with sand and dirt and mud. The masks of hardened dirt on their faces crack when they smile or grimace—the grime shifts with the movement of facial muscles. And even in the youngest of faces is a look of ages-old wisdom that only combat brings. It is a look that says, "You probably wouldn't understand, and I'm not going to tell you anyway." It is a look that can tell heaven from hell: they have seen both.

Sometimes theirs is a look of elation at the prospect of hot chow and a hot shower, two things they have gone without for days or weeks. It is the look of relief at having a break for just a few minutes before the sergeant gives another order.

But if only two or three other marines from their unit are still in the field, you will see in these men's eyes a look of concern and anxiousness. It means that no matter how bad it is in that place with no name—that place identified by just grid coordinates—"We have to get back there right away." Marines never, ever leave their own behind. Never.

Yes, the sight of a fighting marine coming straight from the battlefield is something that, if you ever see it, you will never forget. A photo of these marines is a snapshot of fatigue and camaraderie, quiet determination and heroism. This is seen in photos of marines from every conflict and war since the birth of the Corps in Tun Tavern more than 230 years ago. When you see marines returning from battle, you see a picture of courage and strength unlike any other.

These are the marines I pray *for*.
These are the marines I pray *with*.
These are the marines I have prayed *over*.
There is no finer sight than a marine coming straight from the battlefield.

STRENGTH AND COURAGE

SHAKING OFF THE DUST

"If anyone will not welcome you or listen to your words, shake the dust off your feet when you leave."
—MATTHEW 10:14 NIV

On the Beirut Memorial at Camp Lejeune, North Carolina, a memorial in honor of the 241 marines, sailors, and soldiers killed by a suicide truck bomb in Lebanon in October 23, 1983, four words are written:

THEY CAME IN PEACE

Being a member of the military is dangerous. Often people do not care if our forces are in a foreign land to restore peace to war-torn and terror-torn countries.

Our motives in serving and answering the call of freedom must be pure and peaceful. Even in war, our goal is to achieve peace. War is the last desire of the soldier, sailor, marine, airman, or coastguardsman. In war they pay the highest price. The goal of achieving peace can get lost as war drags on and there are long and hazardous deployments.

Serving in the military is especially difficult when people we serve with are killed or seriously wounded.

We come in peace, but too often we have to shake off the dust of unwelcoming people or insurgencies. It doesn't take much time in the desert to learn how to shake off the dust—literally or metaphorically.

Still, we must continually extend the olive branch of peace, make the effort, and pray.

Prayer may be the only answer for human beings who are historically and constantly at war or in conflict with one another. Perhaps God's answer to our prayers for peace is to let us know that we must be willing for God to use us as he answers that prayer.

Today we shake off the dust and pray. Our motive is peace. Our wish is to return home whole to our loved ones. In Iraq and Afghanistan our troops must learn to live in and shake off the dust. We must all learn to pray for peace and then become an answer to that prayer.

Prayer to Overcome Obstacles

"DIFFICULTIES" IS THE NAME GIVEN TO THINGS
WHICH IT IS OUR BUSINESS TO OVERCOME.
—*Admiral Ernest J. King*

Lord of All Possibilities:
We understand your Word that tells us
we can move mountains.
We understand your Word that proclaims
all things are possible with you.
We have faith the size of a mustard seed that will grow
into the greatest of shrubs.
We will ask in prayer, and you will answer.
We are your people. You are our God.
Though the earth be removed,
If the mountains are carried into the sea,
When the waters roar,
Enemies encamp around us,
Hordes of devils fill the land,
If everything turns against us . . .
We will not fear.
We will overcome all obstacles.
We will be triumphant.
You are our sword and shield.
We carry your promises forward into battle.
We can overcome the greatest of odds.
Give us faith.
Grant us strength.
It is our business to overcome.
Amen.

ADAPT AND OVERCOME

Some amazing examples of faith come from the beliefs and lifestyles of marines. They have an attitude, instilled during basic training and carried on through generations, that makes them the most respected fighting force in the world. Marines believe and live the ethos that there is no challenge so great that they cannot conquer it. They believe that they can adapt and overcome in any situation. Working with these warriors rubs off on me in a spirit of pride and motivation. It is a spirit that serves marines, and it can serve all of us well in any part of our lives.

Jesus said this:

"If ye have faith as a grain of mustard seed, ye shall say unto this mountain, Remove hence to yonder place; and it shall remove; and nothing shall be impossible unto you." —Matthew 17:20

Marines carry faith with them that is strong whether they have served a single four-year tour or an entire thirty-year career. No other branch of the military has a motto comparable to that of the marines: "Once a Marine, Always a Marine."

They have a faith in God, corps, and country that makes them a formidable force. This faith is the glue that holds them together and is the reason that marines exhibit the highest esprit de corps of all the services. In their lifestyle is a lesson for all of us.

After all, what is there in our lives that cannot be overcome with great faith, prayer, our actions, and the help of God and others? The idea of adapting and overcoming is not unique to, nor the invention of, the USMC. The idea is in the promise of Christ found in Matthew 17:20.

How many times have you faced an obstacle in life and put all of your faith, devotion, and abilities to work to overcome the seemingly insurmountable mountain that stands in your path? Our Lord says that such overcoming is possible if you have faith, even if it is faith as small as the tiny mustard seed.

Sometimes I wonder if all of us know how incredible the power of faith really is. I have an idea that too many people rely on their own power to get things done and only call out to God in desperation when all else has failed. That's not faith. That's not even hope. That's faithless, hopeless despair. Perhaps that is why so many warriors engaged in battle know this saying: "There are no atheists in foxholes."

Well, listen closely. We don't have to wait until we have our backs up against the wall or find ourselves in either a real or metaphorical foxhole. All of our obstacles and problems can be overcome when we begin with prayer! The answer to our prayers may not be what we expected or prayed for to begin with, but faith will see us through. Prayer warriors can adapt and overcome with the help of God, the power of prayer, and the truth of the Scriptures.

Nothing is stronger than faithful believers prepared to move mountains. We can adapt and overcome all obstacles in life. Believe it. Pray it. Live it.

Prayer in Challenging Times

OPPORTUNITIES TO FIND DEEPER POWERS WITHIN OURSELVES COME
WHEN LIFE SEEMS MOST CHALLENGING.
—*Joseph Campbell*

Mighty God, Holy Lord,
We live in a challenging time in history. Being a member
of the military presents obstacles and opportunities.
We are challenged by separation from family and friends.
We are challenged by the high tempo and great need
of our unit. Drills, uncertainty, and crisis challenge us.
But, God, we thank you for giving us challenges.
Overcoming these challenges invites us to put
our confidence in you, for in you we know that
we can handle any mission placed before us.
We are strong and resilient men and women.
We are proud Americans.
Challenge us, America. Challenge us, World.
Challenge us, and with each other's help, we'll answer.
Grant us courage, honor, and commitment.
Grant us faith and hope.
That is all we need.
Amen.

TURNING IT OVER TO GOD

Praying during times of conflict can be difficult. How do you clear thoughts of war, danger, and worry from your mind so you can hear God's voice?

If you are a parent with a child or if you are a brother or sister with a sibling at war, how do you overcome the nagging worry and deal with the frightening news reports? If you are on the ground in Iraq or Afghanistan, how do you pray with the sounds, sights, and smells of war around you twenty-four hours a day, seven days a week? It is not easy.

I will give you an example. One Sunday morning I was preparing to go to worship when the call came over the radio that an injured person was being flown to our location at the SSTP. Thoughts of worship were lost as the medical team scrambled in response. Tensions heightened when we heard the helicopter land. In moments the ambulance arrived from the flight line, and a thirty-five-year-old woman was unloaded on a stretcher. She was accompanied by her uninjured mother. The injured woman, replete in her black burka, was the victim of a "grazing gunshot wound" to the head. That is to say, the bullet did not penetrate her forehead, but it did fracture her skull severely and could possibly have caused brain damage.

I gathered details about the woman from our translator. Apparently she and her mother had taken their crop—in this case, dates—to the local market in Fallujah. As they returned, they came to a checkpoint. The truck they were riding in stopped and was then caught in an ambush.

She was an innocent victim. She is the mother of six children.

She may fully recover; she may be impaired for the rest of her life. I will never know the answer to that.

She was sedated and intubated for her flight to Baghdad for further tests and treatment. It was the last time I would see her or her mother.

Her case finished in time so that I could still attend the 11:00 a.m. worship.

I did not attend worship. My heart and mind were not right. What would become of that woman? What about her six children? How should I pray for her? How in the world do I pray for my enemies when they use women as a screen in an ambush?

In the middle of this conflict, how could I possibly hear God's voice?

Praying during times of conflict is difficult. Still, I knew at the time that I must pray, that I should at least prepare and try to pray.

I knew the words of the Bible well, and I remembered the words of God in Psalm 46—"Be still, and know that I am God."

The Lord reminded me to be still and to turn over my uncertainty and worry to him.

Is there something so difficult that I cannot handle it? Surely!

Is there something so difficult that God cannot handle it? Surely not!

When I cannot pray amid the conflict, destruction, and insanity of war, I turn to God. I turn my problems over to him.

I am still. It is not long until I find inner peace. It is not long until I find God in these times of conflict. I am still, and I pray.

Later that evening I go to another worship service and pray for the mother of six and her family. Her situation is now, as it always has been, in God's hands.

Prayer for Strength

DAVID SAID TO THE PHILISTINE, "YOU COME AGAINST ME WITH
SWORD AND SPEAR AND JAVELIN, BUT I COME AGAINST YOU
IN THE NAME OF THE LORD ALMIGHTY."
—*1 Samuel 17:45 NIV*

Our strength comes from the Lord.
When those around us doubt our abilities:
Our strength comes from the Lord.
As life becomes tumultuous:
Our strength comes from the Lord.
We persevere when grief overcomes us:
Our strength comes from the Lord.
When our faith and hope waver:
Our strength comes from the Lord.
Should the evil one tempt us:
Our strength comes from the Lord.

So David triumphed over the Philistine with a sling and a stone;
without a sword in his hand
he struck down the Philistine and killed him.
—1 SAMUEL 17:50 NIV

So be it and amen.

IT'S ALL RELATIVE IN IRAQ

He's real sick," one doctor says to another. Sick? I didn't hear anyone sneeze or cough. When surgeons say that a patient is "real sick," they mean that the person needs surgery right away for a nasty wound, sometimes a life-threatening wound. I'm thinking, *That's not real sick. That's hurt real bad!*

A few days ago I caught myself saying to a doctor, "He's not very sick. He got lucky!"

Lucky? The poor kid got shot in the leg, but all the neurological exams reveal that everything is intact. Another half inch higher, though, and the bullet would have severed major arteries and nerves and most likely snapped his tibia and fibula bones like dry twigs. I told the young marine that he was lucky, and he looked at me like I was crazy!

It's all relative in Iraq. Life or death is often determined by less than an inch, sometimes even by centimeters. How you view life following an injury depends on your position. I'll give you an example.

Recently a soldier came in with intense pain. He was screaming and hollering—and justifiably so. He had just been hit by a rocket-propelled grenade. He had no wound below his knees and none above the tops of his thighs. However, in the mid-thigh range, his legs were destroyed. After he was knocked out and intubated by the anesthesiologist, the team began to unwrap his legs. He would lose his right leg. Even I, the most untrained person in the room, could see that. Perhaps the left leg could be saved. From the top of the leg, that possibility didn't look good. As the surgeons lifted the leg, it was clear there was no way to save this leg either. But now the race

124

was to save his life. A bilateral amputation causes a lot of trauma to the system. The Walking Blood Bank was activated, and this soldier received more than twenty units of blood. Surgery was successful in saving his life. As this nineteen-year-old soldier left our facility, I knew that he faced several surgeries and a long, painful recovery. His life had been forever altered.

As a forty-five-year-old husband and father, I saw him as lucky to be alive. In his place, I would be glad to have the use of my arms to hug my children and my mind intact to tackle projects. I could learn to ski in one of those specially designed chairs, to race in a wheelchair, to drive a car using hand controls, or to skate down the driveway with my youngest ones and not skin my knees. But he is nineteen years old. How does he see his new life? Will he embrace the challenges? Or will he wish he had died on the battlefield?

It's all relative in Iraq.

Relativity. That is probably the biggest change in all of us who serve over here in Iraq. Some normal, everyday things just don't seem very significant to life anymore. Some things that weren't significant before certainly are important now. I'll give you another example.

My wife and I have five amazing children. The first one was in the National Honor Society and went to college on an academic scholarship. The second one is about to be inducted into the National Honor Society. The third is an honor student in middle school. The fourth is at the top of his first-grade class. The fifth may be the smartest of the bunch. One of the biggest reasons they are successful is that my wife, Leigh, is there for them to help with homework, to hear how the day went, to drive them to activities, and to dispense both advice and discipline. They run her ragged most days, but none of them causes real trouble. Five kids are plenty to keep up with. And as much as we love them, we can imagine a day when the house will be quiet. Of course by that time we'll be too old to do much other than smile at each other and let the chairlift help us up from watching TV!

Being in Iraq makes things relevant . . . You see, Leigh and I have a soft spot for kids, and raising kids may be the one thing that we are good at doing. We e-mail back and forth about the beautiful children of Iraq whom I see in such dire straits at our surgical unit. Unlike my last tour in Iraq, the surgical unit is now seeing children every week because of the change in enemy tactics. The medical team now has a fully stocked pediatrics crash cart. So, as Leigh and I e-mail back and forth, it is clear that our time with children is not done. Let me rephrase that: our time of having more children of our own is done, but so many, too many, children right in our own surrounding counties in North Carolina need the one thing we can offer—a loving family. God has made it clear that all the other things we always thought were relevant—things like a big house and cars and nice furniture—aren't relevant at all when you live through a couple of deployments to a war zone. What's relevant on this tour are the little ones I see every week who are in real trouble. I've held the hand of a precious six-year-old boy as he took his last agonizing breaths before he died. I've held the leg of a darling two-year-old as it was amputated and then fashioned her a diaper out of ABD pads. So when I get back from Iraq, we will add to our family either by adoption or by foster care leading to adoption.

One thing Iraq teaches us, each in a unique way, is that all is relevant, and all is relative.

Next time you get a cold and complain about being sick, remember what "real sick" can be. Next time one of your kids gives you a bit of trouble, remember what "real trouble" can be for a child.

It's all relative in Iraq.

Prayer for Courage

"BLESSED ARE YOU WHEN PEOPLE INSULT YOU, PERSECUTE YOU
AND FALSELY SAY ALL KINDS OF EVIL AGAINST YOU BECAUSE OF ME.
REJOICE AND BE GLAD, BECAUSE GREAT IS YOUR REWARD IN HEAVEN."
—*Matthew 5:11–12 NIV*

Lord, give us courage!
Give us courage to stand up for our beliefs
and principles when others dismiss or ridicule us.
Lord, give us courage!
Give us courage when the truth is too close for comfort,
and some of us find ourselves uncomfortable.
Lord, give us courage!
Give us courage to remind one another that we are granted
freedom of religion, not freedom from religion in society.
Lord, give us courage!
Give us courage to be men and women
who speak up for one another at home
and around the globe whenever persecution is present.
Lord, give us courage!
Give us courage to trust that nothing
can separate us from the love of Christ.
Lord, give us courage!
Give us courage to know that our heavenly reward
is greater than any earthly prize.
Lord, give us courage!
Amen.

NO ATHEISTS IN FOXHOLES

Fear is a companion of marines, soldiers, sailors, and airmen whenever they head into combat. In that case, a moderate amount of fear is a good thing. Fear sends a rush of adrenaline into the system that can heighten senses. Fear can make a well-trained warrior depend on the lessons learned in basic training and instincts gained during years of experience. Fear makes warriors remember that they are dependent on a whole team of individuals. Fear makes even the most courageous warriors realize that they are not invincible. Fear also reminds combatants that they do not walk alone and that there is a Force far greater than any set of human allies or enemies. Fear can make privates and generals, seamen and admirals alike turn to God in prayer for protection.

In the Bible, David squared off with a giant named Goliath; Daniel stood unharmed against lions; Shadrach, Meshach, and Abednego stood in a fiery furnace and were not singed; and Paul was bitten by a venomous viper on Malta and suffered no ill effects. God who watched over his servants in Bible times also watches over his children in times of conflict today.

During times of conflict, the strongest and most courageous members of the armed forces turn to God, and their prayers echo the words of David in Psalm 71:1 when he said, "In thee, O LORD, do I put my trust."

And when people put their trust in the Lord, they are reminded of the psalmist's words in Psalm 118:6: "The LORD is on my side; I will not fear: what can man do unto me?"

Paul—who lived through the encounter with the viper, a shipwreck, multiple imprisonments, and constant schemes to take his life—was a fountain of hope that strengthens all who face fear. Foremost among the apostle's writings may be Romans 8:31: "If God be for us, who can be against us?"

It is little wonder that there are no atheists in foxholes. God provides the ultimate comfort and protection from fear during times of conflict. And so we pray for all who face fear by remembering Paul's words in 2 Timothy 1:7 when he says this: "God hath not given us the spirit of fear; but of power, and of love, and of a sound mind."

Prayer in Times of Fear

IF WE ARE STRONG, OUR STRENGTH WILL SPEAK FOR ITSELF.
IF WE ARE WEAK, WORDS WILL BE OF NO HELP.
—*John F. Kennedy* [14]

Lord,
Many times we face danger with trepidation and fear.
Grant us courage.
Remind us that our mission is dangerous but necessary.
As we face peril, impart to us the wisdom to follow leaders who
have conquered both fear
and the enemy in their years of experience.
Give us honor and conviction to step into the breach when
every fiber of our body wants to turn in the other direction.
War must be taken with all seriousness.
Those who have faced death value life even more.
Be with us on the fields of battle. If the battle is long,
filled with darkness and danger, convey to us a sense of
our purpose: we are protecting our nation and freedom.
When we face criticism by those unwilling to pay the price
for this freedom, let us fight that much harder
to secure their right to express their opinions.
Those of us who fight for peace and freedom
call on you for strength and protection.
We pray for all of those who serve with us in times of danger
and all who will follow in our steps, and we pray in honor
of all who have conquered fear and given us freedom.
We also pray with gratitude in memory of those
who have sacrificed their lives.
O Most Holy Lord, we will stand together;
we will stand strong in you.
Amen.

130

COME-TO-JESUS MEETINGS:
Misses, Near Misses, and Good Luck

There is a saying we use with a sense of sarcasm when someone has a close call with the enemy here in Iraq. We call it a "Come-to-Jesus Meeting." Or perhaps, if you'd like a hymn to go with that kind of moment, it would be "Nearer My God to Thee."

Come-to-Jesus meetings fall into three categories: misses, near misses, and good luck.

Misses are a fairly normal occurrence. They happen to every service member in Iraq at one time or another. Misses generally include an indirect fire (IDF) attack. IDF takes the forms of rockets or mortars. Camp Al Taqaddum (TQ), takes occasional IDF attacks, generally in the form of rockets. There is an early-warning system in place that is triggered when radar detects incoming rounds. The warning consists of a broadcast from "The Big Voice," speakers spread throughout camp that give a loud warning: "INCOMING, INCOMING, INCOMING! WARNING! SEEK SHELTER!"

In reality, that announcement may give you as little as ten seconds or as much as twenty seconds to grab your flak jacket and Kevlar helmet, duck into a hardened structure, or get close to a cement or HESCO (sand-filled) barrier. Just the "incoming, incoming, incoming" warning bellowing from the Big Voice can elicit a quick prayer. Often there's just enough time to say, "Oh, Jesus!"

If I am in my office in the Mainside Chapel, I utter a quick prayer as I grab my gear. There is no time to get to a hardened shelter. I pray because

131

I know that this chapel has been hit three times by IDF. On September 30, 2005, for instance, IDF blew out the wall to my office and destroyed a bag of my clean laundry, computer, and books. I was not on base at the time, so there was no come-to-Jesus meeting for me. Still, it really irritated me until I realized that it is better to have your shorts blown up in your laundry bag than on your person. And this type of gallows humor is not unusual in Iraq, but it is not always appreciated by those back home who worry about loved ones out here.

A miss will shake the ground around you and get your attention, but otherwise the attack is not sufficiently close to cause undue concern. A miss causes more curiosity about where the rounds impacted than anything else. However, one person's miss can be another person's near miss.

A near miss is just a matter of geography. My first experience with a near miss was in late October 2005. I was building shelves for our living quarters (a sixteen-by-thirty-two-foot plywood hut shared by six people) with one of my roommates, Lt. Phil Davis, a physician's assistant. In 2005 there was no early-warning system at TQ. Our warning consisted of hearing about the last two seconds of the rocket's approach, the last two seconds before impact. You surely don't forget that whistling sound—at which I simultaneously dropped the wood I was carrying and made eye contact with Phil. There was nowhere to run at that point. The round landed about forty yards away, and that certainly qualifies as a come-to-Jesus meeting. No time for a quick prayer. And (here's more gallows humor) you have to check your skivvies after impact! I found out quickly that I can still run pretty darn fast. You see, it is rare that there is only one incoming round, so we evacuated the area quickly. Luckily, in this case there was only one round, and no one was hurt. It was a nearer miss for the people in a building only ten yards from the site of impact. Fortunately, no one was injured. The prayer after Phil and I stopped running was nearly the same as the one before a miss: "Oh, Jesus, that was close!"

The number of prayers accompanying near misses is directly correlated to the distance from the near miss. And a miss from small-arms fire (SAF) like that from an AK-47 is measured by feet or inches instead of yards from rocket or mortar fire. The brevity and intensity of the prayers accompanying these SAF near misses follow the same rules of proximity.

Good luck can, believe it or not, accompany injury from IDF or SAF.

In my time serving with the Surgical Shock and Trauma Platoon (SSTP), I can give you two examples of good luck that accompanied an injury and the subsequent awarding of a Purple Heart.

The first case involved a religious program specialist (those navy enlisted who are assigned to work with navy chaplains) who was off base with his chaplain and their unit as they conducted a road repair mission. A sniper took a shot just as the young man moved. Judging by numerous sniper victims, we saw clearly that the shot was intended to hit the victim either just under the bottom of his flak jacket or between the protective plates. His movement at the exact same time the shot was fired caused the round to miss his torso and pass through his arm, just above the wrist, as it hung by his side. The wound was a "through and through," barely missing crucial nerves and not shattering the bone. The shot did break the bone severely enough to cause him to be sent home to get it pinned in place, but he was able to walk into the SSTP.

If he had not moved, the shot could have proved fatal. On more than one occasion, I have been called to pray for those who did not survive similar shots. But this sailor had "good luck" even while earning the Purple Heart.

The second case of good luck involved more serious injuries, but the soldier claimed he was "very lucky." The combat outpost near Ramadi was frequently mortared by the enemy in the fall of 2005. After a particularly long day on patrol, a young National Guardsman literally flopped onto the top rack of the bunk bed in his living quarters. Only an hour later the small base took several mortars inside the compound. One of those mortars hit the mud and brick wall (local Iraqi construction that crumbles easily) just above the end of this soldier's bunk. His injuries were substantial. One foot was hit, blown open between the big toe and second toe, tearing the foot nearly halfway down. He was also peppered by fragmentation down the backs of his legs, his buttocks, and his back. The injuries to his foot would require surgery at our SSTP and further surgery in Germany. As he lay on the stretcher in our emergency room, I spoke with him for a few minutes before his surgery.

"You won't believe how lucky I am, Chaplain," he said.

Outside of the fact that he was alive, I found that statement hard to believe. "How's that?"

"Normally I sleep with my head against the end of the bunk by the wall, and I never sleep on my stomach. But today I was so tired that I kinda vaulted into the top rack, swung my feet to the end by the wall, and fell asleep on my stomach. If I had slept like usual, this would have struck my head, and the fragments would have gone into my neck, chest, stomach, and another exposed area farther south."

We chuckled together. "Man, you *are* lucky." He would have been killed instantly had he been in his usual sleeping position.

Then the soldier asked if he could stay with his unit. That would be impossible.

And usually when I tell this story, I have to end by saying, "Swear to God, it's a true story!"

You have to love the spirit of our troops exemplified by these two "good luck" soldiers. Shot and blown up and considering themselves lucky—and both wanted to stay with their units. Simply amazing spirits!

Their prayers after realizing their good luck in the aftermath of combat danger were those of relief and thanksgiving.

They had nearly had a real meeting with Jesus.

As military members in the combat zone, we joke in a way that civilians sometimes don't understand. Perhaps it's a survival or keep-your-sanity mechanism when we're living day to day with danger.

Prayer is involved in a come-to-Jesus meeting whether it is a miss, a near miss, or good luck. We hope to have these prayers of relief and thanksgiving instead of the ones that we have had, on too many occasions, when our brothers and sisters in arms have made the ultimate sacrifice.

Keep praying for all who go in harm's way. We're certainly praying—sometimes more fervently and quickly than others. It's all a matter of geography and timing.

I send this to you all with a prayer of thanksgiving. Today is another day after last night's miss, a rocket that landed a couple of hundred yards away and a second rocket even farther away with no injuries. Amen to that! Amen! And we're still praying.

Prayer for Our Country

AMERICA, AMERICA, GOD SHED HIS GRACE ON THEE.
—*Katharine L. Bates, "America the Beautiful"*

God,
For our country we give thanks.
For spacious skies and amber waves of grain,
We give thanks.
For Maine lobsters, Iowa corn, and Hawaiian pineapple,
We give thanks.
For West Virginia coal, Oregon lumber, and Oklahoma oil,
We give thanks.
For religious freedom and for faith unbound,
We give thanks.
For blessings and hope beyond compare,
We give thanks.
For America the beautiful,
We give thanks.
May you always shed your grace on our country.
Amen and amen.

THE 6th CAG

The LORD gives strength to his people;
the LORD blesses his people with peace.
   —Psalm 29:11 NIV

I flew from Cherry Point, North Carolina, to Iraq with a group of marine reservists from all over the country who have formed a group called the Sixth Civil Affairs Group (6th CAG). The mission of the 6th CAG is to help with Iraqi elections, aid local governments, take damage claims from Iraqis, make monetary reparations, and assume a host of other duties. Like all marines, members of the 6th CAG are armed with M-16s and 9mm pistols.

So in the 6th CAG we see a juxtaposition of strength and peace like the psalmist mentions. The difficult part of the 6th CAG's job is not being USMC warriors, but rather making peace; the difficult part is winning the hearts and minds of the Iraqis. I know that sounds like a lot of propaganda, but theirs is a very real, very difficult, and very dangerous mission. These men and women are headed for places like Ramadi, Hit, and other towns throughout Iraq. Many of these places are sites of recent and intense fighting, so the 6th CAG soldiers are ready to defend themselves at all times. In reality, they would love to keep their weapons at their sides. When they have to use their strength as warriors, their mission is at its weakest point. In fact, the use of force greatly detracts from their mission. Only when their weapons remain holstered and on safety can they show their real strength: creating peace and hope in the chaos of a war zone where women and children live. As I talked with them during their flight to Iraq, I heard in their voices an excitement about being ambassadors of goodwill who could make a difference in a war that is often confusing. Yes, it's confusing even to the troops.

136

Peace, hope, and love—these real strengths are harder to learn. In fact, we are a nation and a humanity that have always known war. Winning the hearts and minds of others takes courage against failure, criticism, and ridicule. It is easy to criticize. It is easy to fight. It is another matter to make wrong things right. It is another matter to be blessed peacemakers in a war- and terrorist-torn country. These are the men and women who, during Operation Iraqi Freedom, helped make possible the constitutional referendum in October 2005 and the national election of December 2005.

Pray for the 6th CAG and all service members who have and who will take on this mission in the future. I don't know how many of them are religious, but they are the embodiment of Psalm 29:11; they are people given strength whose true blessing is peace. They are in a war zone trained as warriors, but their strength is creating peace. Pray for these men and women of the USMC's Civil Affairs Group who are serving in dangerous places. They come with the goal of making peace.

May God be with the marines of the 6th CAG and the people of Iraq who want to live and raise their children in peace.

OUR ROOTS AT HOME

Prayer for Patriots

O SAY, CAN YOU SEE, BY THE DAWN'S EARLY LIGHT,
WHAT SO PROUDLY WE HAILED AT THE TWILIGHT'S LAST GLEAMING,
WHOSE BROAD STRIPES AND BRIGHT STARS,
THROUGH THE PERILOUS FIGHT,
O'ER THE RAMPARTS WE WATCHED,
WERE SO GALLANTLY STREAMING?
AND THE ROCKETS' RED GLARE, THE BOMBS BURSTING IN AIR,
GAVE PROOF THROUGH THE NIGHT
THAT OUR FLAG WAS STILL THERE.
O SAY, DOES THAT STAR-SPANGLED BANNER YET WAVE
O'ER THE LAND OF THE FREE AND THE HOME OF THE BRAVE?
—*Francis Scott Key, "The Star-Spangled Banner"*

Lord, we pray for . . .
All who stand at events and sing the national anthem:
May their glory be in their spirit and not their intonation.

Those who paint tiny flags on their cheeks on the Fourth
of July: Their true spirit shines in their eyes and on their faces.

People adorned with red, white, and blue shirts, shorts, jackets,
pants, and bandanas that represent the Stars and Stripes:

They remind us that we are proud to live in this nation.
Citizens who proudly fly the Red, White, and Blue

in their yards, from their car antennas, on their homes,
and in front of their businesses: Let freedom wave!

Patriots of all ages and backgrounds, city and country,
creed and color: they teach us pride in
"the land of the free and the home of the brave."
Amen.

141

WE ARE PROUD OF WHO WE ARE

We are proud of who we are.
We stand up for what we believe.
We keep our families together.
We trust in God but rely on ourselves.
We do what needs to be done.
We are not afraid.
    —HOMER HICKAM[15]

It is hard to sum up one's ideology, but I think Homer Hickam, in his book *We Are Not Afraid*, has captured the ethos of so many of us who serve in the United States military.

We are proud of who we are. Being proud of who we are as individuals is only a part of the equation for a military member. Each of us strives individually to excel. However, our true strength lies in the collective "we" of each unit and every branch of the service. We are strong because of the incredibly rich heritage and traditions that have been passed down to us through the centuries. We are here to live in and uphold the traditions of people with famous names like Vandegrift, Puller, Nimitz, and Pershing. We also serve in the same manner as those nameless thousands whose resting place is the shallows of the Pacific or the forests of Europe or Korea. It is pride, not pay or fame, that is at the heart of daily service. Pride in our country, respect for tradition, and the desire to take our place alongside our brothers and sisters in arms reside in our spirits. Homer Hickam knows: he is a US Army and Vietnam veteran. We take our place in Iraq, Afghanistan, or wherever we are led. We are just as proud as Americans who fought more than 230 years ago for the independence of this nation.

We stand up for what we believe. This makes us the most valuable asset in the protection of our nation. Not only will we stand up for what we believe, but we will die for it as well. You and I made commitments based

142

on our belief in the value of defending freedom and a way of life. We swore an oath to our country. We joined a particular branch of the service based on what best suited our beliefs and the beliefs of that institution. We have freely given away the right to express our opinions on many matters. We have given away this right for a greater cause: defending others' rights. Our nation—in fact, this world—is a safer place because, through the years, millions of us have stood when others were unwilling or unable.

We keep our families together. In a time when too many sacred values are being treated lightly, are completely lost, or are totally ignored, we hold fast to one of the original values of humanity: the family. We are fortunate that our families extend beyond mothers, fathers, husbands, wives, and children. We also have family described as a unit, a band of brothers, a corps, or a nation. We keep our families together because we cannot survive or thrive on our own. Our immediate families bear the burden of deployments as much as all of us who go in harm's way. Through thick and thin, we do everything in our power to achieve and maintain unity. We may stumble and fall because none of us is perfect, but we get back up again—and usually with the help of our immediate or collective family.

We trust in God but rely on ourselves. There is prayer—and then there is prayer accompanied by action. Which would you choose? We gather immense strength from our God and our spiritual lives, but only we can put into action the talent, strength, and resolve that God has granted to us. Never overlook the fact that you are the answer to many of your own and others' prayers. All the faith in the world is for naught without action. God calls us not just to pray for the world, but to go and make disciples of the world. God calls us not just to pray for our neighbors, but to love our neighbors and treat them as we would want them to treat us.

We do what needs to be done. It's hard to elaborate on the importance of that statement. Whatever it takes . . . wherever it takes us . . . for however long it takes us . . . we get the job done. If we don't do it, who will?

We are not afraid. We serve so that others may live in peace with peace of mind. We do not want to die, yet we do not fear death.

We are proud of who we are. We stand up for what we believe. We keep our families together. We trust in God but rely on ourselves. We do what needs to be done. We are not afraid. I did not write these phrases—I wish I had—but I can live that way each day of my life.

143

Prayer for the Flag

I PLEDGE ALLEGIANCE TO THE FLAG OF THE
UNITED STATES OF AMERICA,
AND TO THE REPUBLIC FOR WHICH IT STANDS,
ONE NATION UNDER GOD, INDIVISIBLE,
WITH LIBERTY AND JUSTICE FOR ALL.

Lord,
I will salute the flag for all who
have lost their right arm in combat.
I will salute the flag for all who have lost their legs in combat
and cannot stand at the beginning of a public event.
I will salute the flag for all the loved ones who sacrifice
as much as the military member does.
I will salute the flag for all who are prisoners of war.
I will salute the flag for all who are missing in action.
I will salute the flag for all who have sacrificed their lives
so that it can fly above a free nation.
I will salute the flag, for I am proud.
I will salute the flag, for I am an American!
Amen.

144

Prayer for the Free

YOU CAN ONLY PROTECT YOUR LIBERTIES IN THIS WORLD
BY PROTECTING THE OTHER MAN'S FREEDOM.
YOU CAN ONLY BE FREE IF I AM FREE.
—*Clarence Darrow*

We thank you, God Almighty, for making us free—
Free to live under the umbrella of your love and grace;
Free to share this love with all people of all races and all places.
We thank you, God Almighty.
When we let this freedom ring, it cannot
be delayed in any corner of our nation.
We thank you, God Almighty.
It is left up to us to spread the message of love, equality,
peace, and justice. But only when we fulfill that great calling
to all of humanity will we be truly free as individuals.
We thank you, God Almighty, for all who have preached,
lived, and died for this message of hope. They are free!
May we join them in a never-ending quest for freedom.
Let it ring in our hearts. Let it ring in our souls.
Let it ring in our words. Let it ring in our actions.
We thank you, God Almighty, for making us free!

THE WARRIOR AND PEACEMAKER

*Seize the initiative with the offensive mind-set of a warrior
and the heart of a peacemaker.*
—MAJOR GENERAL W. E. GASKIN, USMC

This quote is on a card that all of us deploying with the USMC to Al Anbar Province received for this rotation. Major General Gaskin is the commander of the Multinational Forces West and Second Marine Expeditionary Force (II MEF) Forward here in Iraq.

Our rules of engagement have also changed. To be sure, the individual combatants on the ground still have the primary right and responsibility to defend themselves when threatened. Our enemy fights a guerrilla style of warfare and does not abide by any rules. This means our marines, who are the most highly educated marines in history, have to think and react within moments as the enemy hides among the Iraqi people, in mosques, and in schools. Guerrilla warfare also puts those ground forces in a place that their basic training didn't envision five or ten years ago.

One side fights fair (in itself, an odd comment during a war in which both sides set out to kill the other), and the other side uses any means necessary to achieve its goals. IEDs have been planted on dead bodies and animal carcasses, arranged in patchwork on the pavement, attached to guardrails and bridges—the list goes on and on, as you see each night on the evening news. Add to that suicide bombers in cars and on foot, suicide bombers who are females, some even carrying a baby. Rockets and mortars are fired at any target conceivable. How do our marines, sailors, soldiers, and airmen deal with all this and move forward to secure peace?

As you can see, this reality is the challenge I face as one called to take care of the spirits of the men and women who prosecute this war on a daily basis. It is not an easy, straightforward war. It is simultaneously war and an effort to establish government and peace. It is a tug-of-war in the warrior's spirit that perhaps no war to date has been.

I take care of warriors who one day are being blown up by an IED, who the next day have to discern who is a "bad guy" and who isn't, and who the third day are part of a medical mission to bring treatment to local villages, soccer nets to a bare field, or school supplies to an Iraqi elementary school.

The young men and women of our armed forces not only fight the enemy; they also fight a daily conflict within themselves. A vast majority of those who return home will readjust and then be fine. The numbers of actual PTSD (post-traumatic stress disorder) cases are debatable. (Remember that in today's world, numbers equal funding. I wonder where all the PTSD cases from WWII are.) What I do see are what I can only describe as young men and women who are experiencing midlife changes even though they are only, on average, between twenty and twenty-five years old. Being around the constant threat of violence reframes one's priorities in life. The importance of everyday issues changes. Coming back home in one piece gives one a whole new perspective on life.

However, I also deal with another class of warriors: those who have been injured severely or lost a buddy. They have had their lives unalterably changed. Their wounds go deep, to the very core—to their spirits. And they often face a choice: to continue fighting, which is a good thing, or to withdraw and live in the pain. One of the most inspiring things I've ever witnessed is the tears of soldiers, sailors, and marines who have to leave their units due to their wounds. In so many instances their tears are caused not because of their physical pain, but by the realization that they cannot return to their unit and the buddies with whom they have formed an inextricable bond. I witness tears of mourning. In the midst of serious injury, these soldiers are overwhelmed by guilt, an unwarranted but natural sense of guilt that comes with abandoning their unit. That type of loyalty is amazing to me. That type of loyalty is why you see our young men and women stand tall in dress uniforms when they represent their branch of service at an event back home. We represent those who have suffered and sacrificed—here in Iraq and for generations past—to protect freedom.

Each day I get up and walk and talk. I tour the work spaces, and I visit the hospital with the wounded and the morgue where brave marines work to send "angels" back home. When I ask, "How are you doing today?" I am truly asking, "How is your spirit today?" I offer to pray with them, and I talk to God about them more then I ever imagined I would pray!

Winning the war in Iraq is an unconventional and complicated matter. For nearly four years it has been a changing mission. Every day I get up, along with chaplains throughout the war zone, and face the quandary of how to take care of the spirits of warriors ranging from generals to privates. Prayer, Scripture, humor, concern, and the simple act of walking with them is all we can do.

Meanwhile, back home, pray for us and pray for peace—because inside the souls of all these warriors are hearts yearning for peace and for a safe return home when their duty is finished.

Prayer Seeking to Do the Right Thing

HE HATH SHEWED THEE, O MAN, WHAT IS GOOD;
AND WHAT DOTH THE LORD REQUIRE OF THEE,
BUT TO DO JUSTLY, AND TO LOVE MERCY,
AND TO WALK HUMBLY WITH THY GOD?
—*Micah 6:8*

Gracious God,
You are our God.
We are your children.
We are at war, and we seek to do the right thing.
We thank you that yesterday a Muslim man
was operated on by a Jewish surgeon
while a Christian chaplain prayed.
The man receiving surgery was our enemy, yet as one of
your children, he received the very best medical care available.
We ask your help as we continue to bring the best
of ourselves and our values to our jobs every day
so that this war might come to a quicker end.
We humbly pray for the forgiveness of our sins.
Renew in us a right relationship with you and all of humanity.
Watch over us today and teach us to live with grace and mercy.
You are our God.
We are your children.
We are at war, and we seek to do the right thing.
So be it. Amen.

A SIMPLE AND SOLITARY PATH

I read an article recently entitled "The Amish Path to Real Simple." It reminded me of a time not too long ago when I lived in southern Pennsylvania and observed up close the ways of the Amish, who at times seemed caught between their simple ways and the twenty-first century. An example was the ever-curious sight of an Amish horse and buggy parked at the outer edge of the parking lot at a local Food Lion grocery store. Still, I admire the Amish way of life and their intent to simplify life in an effort to remain closer to God.

I even find myself jealous of the Amish when I seem to be "owned" by the things I own. At times I'm also jealous of my brothers in the Chaplain Corps who are unmarried Roman Catholic priests when I am stretched thin trying to be faithful to God and my wife and five children all at the same time. But I am not ready to turn in my Ford Mustang for a horse and buggy, and I can't imagine my life without my family.

I wish at times that I could have lived the simple life of the prophets or disciples who were able to leave everything behind and follow God. In a most unusual twist—being sent to war—I find myself as close as I may ever come to this simple life.

After all, in Iraq my possessions are limited to two seabags and a large backpack. When is the last time any of us lived with only three pairs of shoes? Be honest! I have a pair of shower shoes, a pair of running shoes, and a pair of tan steel-toed combat boots.

But it is not only in my few possessions that I am like those simple-living men of old. I am also related to them by my geographic location. I

150

am not too far from the paths that Jonah begrudgingly followed to Nineveh. I have been to an oasis in the desert that is a holy site for local Iraqis because they believe that Abraham rested there on his journey described in Genesis. The desert, whether in the Middle East or the southwestern United States, has an almost mystical hold over those who take the time to empty themselves of possessions and worries and wander through the sand. Perhaps it is the starkness . . . maybe the quietness . . . or the feeling of smallness in the vast sea of sand.

In the midst of war, in this desert home of ancient Babylon, I continue to see the mystical power of God, who, from ancient times to modern day, leads his people through the sands. I see hardened warriors quietly asking for a Bible. I hear the confessions of scared young men and women who are facing a very real enemy and coming face-to-face with their mortality at an age when most of their peers feel immortal.

It is my calling to point out to them that they are wandering in the desert, keeping fine company with Abraham, Isaac, Jacob, Moses, Jonah, and a host of biblical others including our Lord Jesus Christ—who all spent time seeking, searching, and finding God in this vast desert. What first appeared to be a journey to a wasteland, a journey to a war-filled land, has become a journey with God in the desert.

I can only describe it with what seems to be an oxymoron: a spiritual blessing in the middle of a war.

If any of us ever doubted God's ability to work through any situation, I would just tell those people to wander a little in the sand with me—and a host of biblical others—and pray. It is a simple and solitary path . . . and, for me, a blessing.

LIFE IN THE DESERT

Prayer for Justice

SAY YE TO THE RIGHTEOUS, THAT IT SHALL BE WELL WITH HIM:
FOR THEY SHALL EAT THE FRUIT OF THEIR DOINGS.
WOE UNTO THE WICKED! IT SHALL BE ILL WITH HIM:
FOR THE REWARD OF HIS HANDS SHALL BE GIVEN HIM . . .
THE LORD STANDETH UP TO PLEAD,
AND STANDETH TO JUDGE THE PEOPLE.
—Isaiah 3:10–11, 13

Just and Forgiving Lord,
The world longs for justice, and you cry out:
"Pray for your enemies!"
People die at the hands of others, and you pray:
"Father, forgive them."
I wonder how to live in these times, and you hail:
"I am the way!"
It is difficult as we strive to do your will,
and you remind me: "The way is narrow."
I am quick to condemn, and you tell me:
"Whatever you do to the least of these you do unto me."
Your requirement of justice seems
much harder than an eye for an eye.
Extending mercy is far more difficult than seeking revenge.
To walk humbly contradicts the
fame and fortune valued in this world.
And yet I would ask you for justice and mercy on the final day.
Forgive my sins. Soften my heart.
Heal my wounds and prejudices.
O Lord of justice, it is a challenging and complicated life.
Hear our prayers, O Lord.
Amen.

Prayer for Mercy

HEAR ME WHEN I CALL, O GOD OF MY RIGHTEOUSNESS:
THOU HAST ENLARGED ME WHEN I WAS IN DISTRESS;
HAVE MERCY UPON ME, AND HEAR MY PRAYER.
—Psalm 4:1

Merciful God,
In times of distress we ask for protection;
Have mercy on us.
In times of abundance we ask for continued blessing;
Have mercy on us.
Your foolishness is wiser than our wisdom,
your weakness stronger than our strength;
Have mercy on us.
All the days of our lives belong to you;
Have mercy on us.
You cover us with blessings;
Have mercy on us.
Humbly we pray;
Have mercy on us.
Have mercy on us.
Have mercy on us.
Amen.

PRECIOUS DAY

Today is a precious day.

When it is gone, we will never get it back.

So let us pray for the important and priceless things in life.

We will pray for our families and friends.

Our churches and neighborhoods.

Our Corps, our Navy.

Our country.

There is no better prayer than one of thanksgiving for all our blessings.

We pray that our struggle and sacrifice will bring freedom to the people of Iraq so that they, too, will see the need to begin each day in thanksgiving.

We pray to remain safe, strong, and courageous so that we may protect those people and ideals most precious to us.

Today is a precious day.

If there is only one thing that I'll take away from working with the Surgical Shock Trauma Platoon and with Mortuary Affairs, it would be that life is precious. Quality of life is subject to perspective, but life is uncertain in any war. Each day should be treated as a gift from God.

Prayer for Forgiveness

CAIN SAID TO HIS BROTHER ABEL,
"LET'S GO OUT TO THE FIELD."
AND WHILE THEY WERE IN THE FIELD,
CAIN ATTACKED HIS BROTHER ABEL
AND KILLED HIM.
—*Genesis 4:8 NIV*

Forgiving Lord,
Since the beginning of time, humans have hardened their
hearts. We have held grudges and hurt one another. At times
our rage and callousness consume the soul. You have tried to
teach us, and too often we have failed to learn.
Forgive us of jealousy.
Forgive us of greed.
Forgive us of anger.
Forgive us of hatred.
Forgive us of violence.
Forgive us of murder.
Teach us the lessons of Cain and Abel.
We humans have hurt one another far too long.
Fill our souls with forgiveness, patience, respect,
contentment, and love. Renew our minds.
Let us break the cycle of hardened hearts.
We humbly ask your forgiveness.
Amen.

WAR AS A NONCOMBATANT

By the regulations of the Geneva Convention and the long tradition of priests and clerics on the battlefields, military chaplains are noncombatants. I operate within the institutions of the United States Navy and the United States Marine Corps, whose members are trained to fight and, when necessary, kill the enemy. But something pulls rank over the military. You see, I am subject first to the teachings and practices of the holy gospel. In many instances those two sets of guidelines run headlong into each other. I'll cite two examples.

As an ordained Christian pastor, I am called on by Christ to echo his words in the Gospel according to Luke, who in chapter 6 wrote this:

> But I say to you who hear: Love your enemies, do good to those who hate you, bless those who curse you, and pray for those who spitefully use you. To him who strikes you on the one cheek, offer the other also . . . But love your enemies, do good, and lend, hoping for nothing in return; and your reward will be great, and you will be sons of the Most High. For He is kind to the unthankful and evil. Therefore be merciful, just as your Father also is merciful. —Luke 6:27–29, 35–36 NKJV

During predeployment training at Camp Lejeune, everyone in attendance is given a small card with the rules of engagement guide printed on it. Later, when I land in Kuwait, I am given the same card again. Across the top of that pocket-sized card in bold print appears the following statement, which is in direct contradiction to what Jesus says in the gospel of Luke: "Nothing on this card prevents you from using deadly force to defend yourself."

It's not just in battle that I am confronted with this dilemma. While stationed as the chaplain at Camp David, I am asked to pray for a solution to what appears, according to all news reports and rhetoric, to be an impending war. There is a sinking feeling that the solution will not come peacefully. In fact, only two can truly answer this prayer request. One is God almighty, for whom nothing is impossible; the other is the president, who will ultimately make the decision to keep the military in reserve or send them into battle.

It's not long before we are at war, and I stand at the front of a congregation that includes the president, my commander in chief, who has made the decision to send our troops and our nation to war in Iraq. Never before have I faced this great a challenge in ministry. Before March 23, 2003, I had not ministered to persons during times of war or with units actually involved in the fighting. That challenge stretched my pastoral and theological stances. Two and a half years later, in August 2005, I am stationed with marines and sailors in Iraq. Now I will minister to combatants in a war zone. I will minister in the deadly areas of Iraq known as the Sunni Triangle and the Al Anbar Province.

During times of peace and especially during times of war, I am called to be a messenger of peace and forgiveness; I am even called to pray for those who would try to kill me and those around me. Chaplains are the only ones present in military uniform who do not carry weapons. Even our doctors are issued sidearms to protect themselves or their patients should the need ever arise.

What many people outside of the military do not see or realize is that the marines and sailors with whom I serve in Iraq expect and demand that I fill the role of a noncombatant. And while these marines and sailors are willing to serve and fulfill their roles in this war, they would have rather seen a diplomatic and peaceful solution to our problems. When we go to war, these men and women risk their lives and are separated from their families and friends.

So I will and must continue to advocate for peace and pray for my enemies.

It is what God calls me to do.

It is what the military expects me to do.

My greatest challenge is to remain faithful to God when those with whom I serve are on the battlefield and there are enemies around me who would try to kill me.

I am a Christian chaplain.

I am a noncombatant. If I do not stand for peace, forgiveness, and reconciliation in Iraq, who will?

HESCO BEACH:
THE LIGHTER SIDE OF WAR

You don't survive being in a war zone more than six thousand miles from home for six months to a year without a sense of humor and camaraderie. Every unit in every service has ways of relaxing and blowing off steam. For the doctors assigned to the Surgical Shock Trauma Platoon (SSTP) at Taqaddum, the location for relaxation is HESCO Beach.

HESCO Beach is not actually a beach. Oh yes, there is plenty of sand, but there is no water. HESCO Beach is an elevated gathering point replete with folding beach chairs, a canopy of camouflage netting, Christmas tree lights for nighttime festivities, a railing so one doesn't fall off the seven-and-a-half-foot drop from the top, a ladder to climb onto the elevated beach, a boom box to supply music, and a small area of Astroturf to hit golf balls.

HESCO Beach is so named because it is built on top of numerous HESCO barriers (HESCO is the company that produces the barriers). These barriers, which come in a variety of sizes, are canvas bags enclosed in heavy-gauge wire mesh and filled with sand. When filled, they are placed together tightly by a forklift or bulldozer to form a barrier next to tents and buildings, and these barriers absorb the blast from rocket or mortar attack. They do a more than adequate job in that military function.

The doctors in the last rotation have added to this military use by smoothing sand across the top and using the HESCO barriers as a platform for their beach. The barriers' location is further enhanced by its view of the flight line.

During slow periods between casualties, individuals or groups climb the ladder to HESCO Beach in order to escape, catch up on paperwork,

162

have a cup of coffee, read, swap stories of the day, drink nonalcoholic beer, smoke cigars, or listen to music. Friendships are formed, laughter is heard, and every now and then, the war is forgotten, even though helicopters and C-130s constantly take off and land within sight.

There are other places at Taqaddum to relax: other units have places such as the Black Sheep Coffee Shop, the Bada-Bing, or the swimming pool (actually a four-foot-deep converted fuel bladder).

There are more ways to take care of one's spirit than just religion and prayer. Laughter is often termed "the best medicine." Bibles aren't required at this spiritual retreat, only a good sense of humor. Just ask the group watching when a doctor teed off at HESCO Beach with a 7 iron and almost took out the commanding general's judge advocate general (JAG) officer as he rounded the corner.

CHILDREN DURING WAR

Prayer for Innocence

THEN WERE THERE BROUGHT UNTO HIM LITTLE CHILDREN,
THAT HE SHOULD PUT HIS HANDS ON THEM, AND PRAY:
AND THE DISCIPLES REBUKED THEM.
BUT JESUS SAID, SUFFER LITTLE CHILDREN,
AND FORBID THEM NOT, TO COME UNTO ME:
FOR OF SUCH IS THE KINGDOM OF HEAVEN.
AND HE LAID HIS HANDS ON THEM, AND DEPARTED THENCE.
—*Matthew 19:13–15*

Lord,
We are taught as children to share—to share from a box of
sixty-four crayons with a sharpener on the side, to share
amazing toys that we just received at Christmas, or to share a
pile of delectable and colorful Skittles or M&Ms. We have
found great joy in sharing our most prized possessions with one
another. Best of all, we learned to share love, hugs, bedtime
stories, and good-night kisses. As we grow, we are taught to be
more cautious—cautious about those who would look at our
answers during a test, cautious of strangers, cautious of those
who don't look like us, dress like us, live like us, worship like us.
We find isolation in so much caution. Worst of all
we lose our innocence, trust, and faith in one another.
Lord, bring back our hope and faith.
Lord, bring back our laughter and spontaneity.
Lord, bring back our sharing and caring.
Lord, bring us a balance of adult wisdom
and childlike innocence.
Lord, let us share the most important moments in life.
Lord, let us come to you as children . . . as your children.
Amen.

ISMAEL

There are many stories from Iraq that never make it to the news. This is one of them . . .

At age eleven, Ismael became the provider for his family. By this tender age, he had lost both of his parents. His mother had been killed during an insurgent attack, and then several months later his father was killed by an improvised explosive device in Habinayah. At an age and a time when any child would be grieving and at a loss without either a mother or a father, young Ismael was forced to find work to support his grandmother and his little sister.

As fate would have it, the US Army Camp at Habinayah was seeking local laborers to perform odd tasks around the base, tasks ranging from picking up trash to filling sandbags. Ismael knew that the minimum age for laborers on the camp was sixteen. Undeterred, he showed up with a falsified identification that listed his age as sixteen.

Now, I don't know what this bold young man looked like at age eleven, but when I met him recently at age thirteen, he didn't appear to be even that old. So when he was eleven, it was readily apparent that his ID was a forgery, and the Army pulled him aside. A spot of good fortune and his cute smile kept Ismael from being summarily thrown off the base. His luck came in the form of a translator from the base who had raised children of her own. She quickly heard the story of how Ismael had become the man of the family by default. Her heart went out to this determined little boy. His infectious smile immediately softened the hearts of the soldiers, some of whom had children the same age.

168

Nine dollars a day doesn't seem like much for a day's work. However, for an eleven-year-old trying to make money for his family in the Al Anbar Province of western Iraq, it must seem like a small fortune. There is no such thing as the minimum wage in Iraq. I don't even know if there are many child labor laws. Those are moot points when you are eleven years old and trying to survive from day to day and even from meal to meal. Nine dollars a day can save your life—and those of your grandmother and little sister.

When the translator found out why Ismael had lied about his age, she took pity on him. So did those who were hiring laborers for the base. How could anyone do otherwise for this slightly built young man with a head full of dark brown hair and a big grin? To turn him away would be to admit that the war had taken all compassion out of everyone involved. Ismael left that day with a stern lecture about lying. He also left with a job.

Over a year and a half later, Ismael had his life saved a second time by the people stationed in Habinayah. Ismael showed up for work on November 30, 2005, in obvious pain. Afraid of losing his job, he did not complain and said only that he had a stomachache. Later that day, Ismael was still in pain, so the workers took him to the Army aid station. A quick exam by the medic revealed abdominal pain and a fever. Ismael was quickly hustled across the local highway to Camp Al Taqaddum and evaluated by an Army physician's assistant. After twenty-four hours of observation, the ailing young Iraqi was taken to the base's level-two trauma facility with a preliminary diagnosis of appendicitis. The Navy staff at the level two confirmed the diagnosis through exams and blood work.

Ismael was not quite out of the woods. Once the radio calls went out that he was taken to the level-two treatment facility, those in charge of area military medicine wanted to know if the boy was covered for medical treatment by his work as a government contractor.

A government contractor? A thirteen-year-old boy? Winning the hearts and minds of the local population sometimes means cutting through red tape. A call came to the SSTP to determine if his ailment was life-threatening and if his contract covered the procedure. With verbal skills as sharp as his scalpel, the physician in charge of the SSTP informed the powers that be that a rupture and the ensuing sepsis would be life-threatening and that he assumed that, as a contracted worker, Ismael was covered. Besides, he was already headed to surgery and couldn't be sent to a civilian hospital far

169

from his home. In actuality the physician was right: the condition can be life-threatening if left untreated. That stretched the truth a little. But we all knew that as a day laborer, Ismael was not covered by the contracting agents. Furthermore, to be quite honest, he hadn't yet made it to surgery; he was still having blood drawn and IV lines hooked up. The rules would also say that we can treat injured civilians, but standard medical care for noninjured is done at an Iraqi hospital. But the lead physician as well as the ER staff and myself all knew Ismael's story, and there was no way we were sending him to another facility where he may or may not be treated either in time or with the goal of his keeping his job and returning to his family quickly.

So in a matter of minutes, Ismael was taken to the operating room, and the appendectomy was performed. The surgery revealed a gangrenous appendix more serious than the exam workup indicated. It was fortunate that the lead physician stretched the facts and was able to take care of this precious child quickly. Just hours after the surgery, I looked in on the boy to see how he was doing. Not surprisingly, he was being cared for by a trio of our female corpsmen, two of whom have children and the other with one of the biggest hearts of the entire staff. Ismael was grinning from ear to ear, and I couldn't help but think how these women, probably the age of his deceased mother, brought into his life some tenderness that he had been missing.

Sometimes winning hearts and minds means providing a job and medical care to those who may seem of the least significance to the military effort. Winning hearts and minds can also mean breaking more than one of the rules and having compassion. It is doing the right thing when you're in a place where so many things go wrong. And it is a direct bull's-eye of Matthew 18:5 (NIV) says "Whoever welcomes a little child like this in my name welcomes me."

You probably won't hear or read about stories like these. You don't even receive a quarter of the picture of what happens on a day-to-day basis outside of Baghdad. We are only forty-five miles from Baghdad and not far from Fallujah or Ramadi. I continue to see heart-breaking stories just like Ismael's, where boys suddenly become the heads of households. At the same time, I see the inadvertent dangers of living in a country at war. War lies at the heart of both of these stories. As beautiful as Ismael is, his father was taken by this war.

I continue to pray for peace so that there will be no more young children deprived of families or old men wounded while simply driving the highways and byways of their own nation.

Only peace will end these problems. Then and only then will we win the hearts and minds of the Iraqi people. Peace. Pray for peace . . . and for Ismael.

Prayer for the Children of Iraq

My wife, Leigh, sent me an e-mail with pictures of our kids' first day of school and my son, Will, in the pool. The photos made me think, remember, and pray.

During our military briefs about the enemy and convoys, I hear one unusual tip: when the children in a local area are not playing in their usual spots or if they are playing and suddenly scatter to safety in their homes, be alert. This may indicate the presence of a bomb, insurgents, or an ambush. Watch to see if the kids scatter or if they are absent from their normal playgrounds. How incredibly unfortunate and inhumane a comment like this is. It is necessary, but still unfortunate. Think how we grow up in the United States. The Iraqi children are living through a war. I am in their country. And so I offer this prayer.

TRAIN UP A CHILD IN THE WAY HE SHOULD GO,
AND WHEN HE IS OLD HE WILL NOT DEPART FROM IT.
—*Proverbs 22:6 NKJV*

Lord . . . Children are playing in the streets when shots ring out.
Lord . . . Children are riding in cars when IEDs detonate.
Lord . . . Children are waiting anxiously for their fathers—who
are seeking work as a policemen—to return home today.
Lord . . . Children have seen violence
that no one, young or old, should see.
Lord . . . Children have lost parents, siblings,
aunts, uncles, and grandparents.
Lord . . . Children have lost their childhood.
Lord . . . I pray for the children of Iraq, who
live with uncertainty, fear, and death.
Lord . . . Protect them in your loving care.
May they one day know the way of peace.
Amen, Lord. Amen.

172

CHILDREN ARE NOT COLLATERAL DAMAGE

I am reminded today of my two youngest children—Will, who is seven years old, and Erin, who is five. Now, on most days I think a lot about my children, so in that regard today is no different.

But today *is* different. I think of Will and Erin because we had wounded Iraqi children come into our Surgical Shock Trauma Platoon (SSTP) today who were seven and five years old.

The mind has a clever way of getting you through catastrophic events. So I watch the team of doctors, nurses, corpsmen, and even the interpreters to make sure that they are holding up against the daily onslaught of war wounded that is punctuated by the presence of children. In fact, this is the third child with severe wounds to cross our doorstep in less than a week.

In a heartbreaking experience—one that veterans of war never forget— a six-year-old blast victim had one arm and the other hand amputated earlier this week. That child's life was altered forever. A future of what could be was shattered like a china doll dropped onto a hard tile floor.

Today, though, I watch to see if the medical team is holding up well, and I do not focus as much on the children. I get through these cases—the seven-year-old with fragmentation from a mortar lodged in his jaw and the five-year-old suffering a gunshot wound to the torso.

It is only when, hours later, I receive the mail and pictures my wife has sent of our children that I begin to come unraveled. I smile and fight back the tears—tears born of being thousands of miles away from my children. I see their smiles, and I know they are safe. Not soon after, though, I fight back tears of profound sorrow that weigh down my soul—tears for three innocent

173

Iraqi children whose delicate little bodies have been savagely torn apart by the inhumanity of humankind.

Children are not collateral damage.

Children of one culture are no less valuable than children of another.

Those immutable truths should remind us of Jesus' words, "Inasmuch as ye have done it unto one of the least of these my brethren, ye have done it unto me"(Matthew 25:40 KJV). The words of Jesus should not just echo as though our minds were some dank, old cavern. The words of Jesus should slap us across the face, stinging and leaving a sharp, red mark. That would be getting off lightly compared to the wounds of the children I saw today.

I am glad that I have an office to myself as I sit in silence and let the tears stream down my cheeks.

Most days speed by, and I am one of the most upbeat people you will meet. It is my job to tend to the morale of others. But this evening I am deeply saddened, and that sadness is gradually being replaced by anger—anger that you won't see any pictures of wounded children on television. This war is a media-controlled event. The media has its role. As my anger boils over in righteous indignation, I know that none of us comes away clean—none of us walks away without blood on our hands—the blood of children on our hands from this war.

I am hoping that this is hard for you to read. By God, it ought to be hard to read!

God's beautiful children are being caught in the cross fire, in the indiscriminate killing of war. And I don't come out of this any cleaner than anyone else. Being a noncombatant does not exempt me from one iota of responsibility.

Our troops do the best they can to avoid hurting children. They will even put themselves in harm's way to scoop up a child caught in a sudden firefight. But there are accidents, ricochets, and the constant urban warfare.

Back home you may know these far-off cities by name: Baghdad, Mosul, Ramadi, Fallujah, Rahwah, Basra.

Urban warfare means fighting an enemy that has no regard for those around them. Schools pose an opportunity to take advantage of our weakness—our conscience—so they make a good screen for the enemy.

Urban warfare means children living in fear, children in tears, children orphaned, children wounded, and—God forgive us all—children killed.

174

I will have to square my presence here in Iraq—my life in the military—with my soul and my God. That is my own penance to pay.

For today, pray for three little children. It is what you should do. It is all you can do.

In a response to sending out the piece above, I received the following e-mail from a doctor with combat experience whom I've seen save the lives of children:

> Seriously, the kids are tough. But there is a flip side.
>
> During my first deployment to Iraq in 2005, a Bradley [Army fighting vehicle] brought in a skinny little boy, maybe seven or eight, getting CPR. We took him to the OR, with a predictable outcome. (Coming in with CPR nearly always indicates death.) I went back out to ask the soldiers what had happened. They said he was a bad guy.
>
> "He's a little kid. How do you know he was a bad guy?"
>
> "He was pointing an RPG [rocket-propelled grenade] at us from an overpass, so we shot him."
>
> While that boy may have been a "victim of society," it doesn't give him the right to kill anyone else. *That* is why we should be there. Some societies need to be changed.

In the span of the last two weeks, the matter of children in the Surgical Shock Trauma Platoon has intensified. Two brothers, ages four and six years old, are brought in to the SSTP. I have spent over eight months with surgical units, and I know immediately that the fate of these two children has already been decided. It was decided at the point of the IED (improvised explosive device) blast. The six-year-old is rushed to surgery with barely a sign of life, and despite the intense efforts of the medical team, he dies in a matter of minutes. His little brother is in worse shape. He has come in with no discernible vital signs. He never leaves the emergency room section, and last-ditch efforts, including heart massage, fail. When he is rolled over, the team finds an entrance wound in his back that would have proved fatal at even the best hospitals in the world.

As hard as this is to witness as a chaplain—and I also took their father to view his sons after their deaths—I know this is even harder for the medical team. Death is always the enemy of a group of combat surgeons. Death is even harder to accept when children are killed by a cowardly enemy that has no regard for these children.

One week later to the day, a four-year-old and her eight-year-old sister are brought in with injuries: a peppering by IED fragments, a broken wrist, and, most significant, wounds to the head. I see that the older sister will lose sight in one eye. We won't know the extent of the injuries. The SSTP at TQ is a level-two treatment facility and does not have a CT scanner. The sisters are carefully evaluated, intubated, and packaged (kept warm) for further transport to a level-three hospital in Balad, Iraq.

I just hope that none of you ever hear the kind of cries I heard from those two beautiful little girls. I have four daughters, and I was struck to the core by their cries and pleas. I do not speak Arabic, but all you have to do is hear the pain in their tiny, weak voices. That translates, like a dagger through the heart and soul, in any language.

For one of the only times during my service to the SSTP, I have to turn away and gather myself emotionally. I am thankful to God that the doctors, nurses, and corpsmen do such an amazing job. They cannot turn away. Some of them have what my surgeon friend calls "the Mommy factor," the ability to work compassionately with children.

In the span of two weeks, I have witnessed two deaths, a double amputation, a gunshot to the torso, and three critical head wounds to children between the ages of four and eight. This is but one of numerous facilities throughout western Iraq. I shudder to think of those who died right where they were hit, who are lying in the sand and dirt. What about the rest of Iraq?

All these children—the dead, the wounded, and even the boy shooting a rocket-propelled grenade from an overpass—are victims of society. They are victims of adults who have lost positive control of life, and on that point I agree with the doctor when he says that no one has the right to kill. Call it society if you wish. But one thing is certain: in every one of these cases, the child is a victim.

Some children gave their lives because of adults' inability to coexist peacefully. And maybe we've become numb to the plight of children who, during my lifetime, have died in fighting in Vietnam, Cambodia, Iraq,

Kuwait, the Balkans, and the Sudan and as a result of terrorist actions in Russia, the Philippines, Bali, the Twin Towers in New York City, and the Murrah Federal Building in Oklahoma City.

I am finishing this reflection on Ash Wednesday 2007. In a part of the worship service today, I read the following to the worshippers: "Historically the season of Lent provided a time in which converts to the faith were prepared for holy baptism. It was also a time when those who, because of notorious sins, had been separated from the body of the faithful were reconciled by penitence and forgiveness and restored to the fellowship of the church."

I am convicted by the words I read: "notorious sins." Because of notorious sins I must rely on God's forgiveness. As people at war, we all must. In the case of dead and wounded children, we need a lot of forgiveness.

I pray to God that these children are not forgotten by world leaders as a cruel result of war.

I pray to God that you never see or hear the suffering firsthand. (Some who read this have. Pray for them.)

I continue to pray to God for peace.

I am sure that one of the answers to these prayers comes from God when he says, "What did you do for these children? What did you do for peace?"

I hope there is not a condemning silence in response.

I am certain and afraid that in the next eleven months of ministry at the SSTP, I will see more children. If I ever get used to the sight of them in such a place, in such conditions, then God and the Marine Corps and the Navy need to send me home . . . I will have lost my heart and soul.

Prayer for Anxious Times

"I'M LEAVING YOU WELL AND WHOLE.
THAT'S MY PARTING GIFT TO YOU. PEACE.
I DON'T LEAVE YOU THE WAY YOU'RE USED TO BEING LEFT—
FEELING ABANDONED, BEREFT.
SO DON'T BE UPSET. DON'T BE DISTRAUGHT."
—*John 14:27* MSG

Lord,
I walk this life with you, Lord.
Peace like a river runs through my soul.
My heart is content when the world is anxious with worry.
I am not abandoned. I am not alone.
I walk this life with you, Lord.
My spirit is whole, filled with your blessings.
I will lift your name when the earth rumbles
and mountains fall into the sea.
I will remember your presence when
I am successful beyond my dreams.
I walk this life with you, Lord.
Be still, my soul.
Be filled with peace.
I am whole. I am well.
I walk this life with you, Lord.
Amen

178

ANXIOUS TIMES

I see the look in their eyes. They might have been fearful on the streets of Ramadi, but there they could defend themselves. On the streets of Iraq, troops have some control over their situation no matter how desperate it becomes. But in the emergency room tent, the eyes of a wounded marine, soldier, sailor, airman, or Iraqi troop are filled with anxiety.

At an opportune moment when the doctor or nurse steps away, I step in and identify myself as the chaplain. My presence allows their anxiety to come to the surface, and then I hear the questions:

"Am I going to be okay?"

"Will I lose my foot?"

"I can't feel anything in my hand. What's wrong?"

The most poignant question is heard before they head off into surgery: "Will I wake up?"

When a soldier or marine asks, "Will I wake up?" I can see and feel the very real fear of death. This is one of the hardest moments I experience with these brave warriors. I tell them that I will be with them in the operating room and with them when they wake up after surgery.

When I am with wounded Iraqis, I ask the translator to tell them that I am here to pray for them and that I'll be there when they wake up. They look toward me and see the cross on my uniform. At this moment it doesn't matter that I am a believer of a different religion. I give them a nod, a smile, and a thumbs-up. I receive a thumbs-up in return.

At these moments the very real presence of God is felt among us.

Later, when patients are taken from surgery to the postoperative area of the tent, I am there when they wake up. In the daze and confusion of their waking up, I bend over and talk quietly right into their ears. I let them know that I am the chaplain, that surgery went well, and that they will be okay. Even though they are under the effects of the anesthesia, I receive a smile, and they reach out a hand. A simple touch is a connection with the living world.

God is present, and I am the messenger who echoes the words of Christ found in John 14:27 (NKJV): "Peace I leave with you, My peace I give to you . . . Let not your heart be troubled, neither let it be afraid."

The look in their eyes is different now. Anxiety has turned to peace. In a war zone, this is a blessing.

THE WORK OF PRAYER

Prayer for Human Conflict

JESUS SAID UNTO HIM, THOU SHALT LOVE THE LORD
THY GOD WITH ALL THY HEART, AND WITH ALL THY SOUL,
AND WITH ALL THY MIND. THIS IS THE FIRST AND
GREATEST COMMANDMENT. AND THE SECOND IS LIKE UNTO IT,
THOU SHALT LOVE THY NEIGHBOUR AS THYSELF.
—*Matthew 22:37-39*

Lord Jesus Christ,
You call us to love God and our neighbor.
We have failed too many times.
You call us to love God and our neighbor.
Yet again you give us another chance.
You call us to love God and our neighbor.
How will we succeed?
You call us to love God and our neighbor.
We will begin with love.
You call us to love God and our neighbor.
Let us practice these commands.
You call us to love God and our neighbor.
Your life shows us the way.
You call us to love God and our neighbor.
Your teaching reveals the truth.
You call us to love God and our neighbor.
We try; we can. This is our prayer.
Amen.

A BULLET HAS NO CONSCIENCE

A bullet has no conscience.

A bullet is no respecter of nationality, creed, or color.

A bullet tears through a Kevlar helmet and flesh alike.

A bullet can break, splinter, or ricochet off bone.

A bullet can end the life of a man in his prime.

A bullet can end the life of a child before she has had a chance to really live.

A bullet can blind, paralyze, or mutilate.

A bullet does not know.

A bullet does not care.

A bullet does not even kill.

A bullet is only as effective as the one who takes it from the box, loads it, aims, and pulls the trigger.

A bullet has no conscience. Only people do . . . sometimes.

During my time at the Surgical Shock Trauma Platoon and Mortuary Affairs in Iraq, I have seen plenty of GSWs (gunshot wounds). I have seen a GSW where the bullet passed straight through the soldier's body (a through-and-through wound) in a place that caused no damage and required only a washout. I have seen where a bullet entered an arm and ran down the length of it, breaking the bones in several places. I have seen incredibly small fragments of a bullet leave wounds no bigger than a bug bite, yet those tiny wounds severed the nerves and rendered a hand useless. I have seen a GSW from a .50 caliber round that tore a savage hole through the body and wreaked havoc like nothing you can imagine. I have also seen the results of snipers who deftly placed bullets through necks, Kevlar helmets, and other exposed areas; these bullets caused certain death.

In all of these injuries and deaths, the people on the receiving end never knew what hit them. It was not the work of the bullet or the gun. For that matter, it was not even the work of the gunsmith or manufacturer. The bullet and gun sit idle until a human picks them up, loads, takes the safety off, aims, and fires.

Herein lies the dilemma, the problem, and the answer: humanity. Humanity has been killing and at war since Cain killed Abel. Christ was crucified. Men and women die in Iraq every day. It is not just the bullet that has no conscience.

Pray for humanity.

Prayer for My Enemies

BUT LOVE YE YOUR ENEMIES, AND DO GOOD,
AND LEND, HOPING FOR NOTHING AGAIN;
AND YOUR REWARD SHALL BE GREAT,
AND YE SHALL BE THE CHILDREN OF THE HIGHEST:
FOR HE IS KIND UNTO THE UNTHANKFUL AND TO THE EVIL.
—*Luke 6:35*

O God,
I pray for my enemies.
I do not want to be filled with hatred and a hardness of heart.
I pray for my enemies.
I can find no other way to heal the wounds
in my soul caused by war.
I pray for my enemies.
Doing so can run counter to the mission
of the military that I work with.
I pray for my enemies.
Bombs and bullets have not made them go away.
I pray for my enemies.
I do not want to, but I must.
I pray for my enemies.
Grant me courage and strength, O God.
I pray for my enemies . . .
so that we might live in peace.
So be it and amen.

186

PRAY FOR YOUR ENEMIES

Ye have heard that it hath been said, Thou shalt love thy neighbour,
and hate thine enemy. But I say unto you, love your enemies,
bless them that curse you, do good to them that hate you,
and pray for them which despitefully use you, and persecute you;
that ye may be the children of your Father which is in heaven.
—MATTHEW 5:43–45

I have seen firsthand what our enemies can do and are willing to do. I have visited the injured, prayed with the dying, and conducted memorial services for those who have been killed. And yet I am called to pray for my enemies.

When civilians are purposefully chosen as targets in order to send a message of terror, when innocent women and children are killed, I am still called to pray for my enemies.

Day after day the wounded pass through the doors of the Surgical Shock Trauma Platoon and Mortuary Affairs where I am stationed, and still I am called to pray for my enemies.

I cry out to God, "How long, O Lord? How long?"

I ask God to end this war, and he tells me to pray for my enemies.

I wear a cross on my uniform to work every day. I am the person in the midst of these warriors who represents this radical gospel ethic. There are times when I question God. There are times when we all question God. There are doubts and frustrations.

Praying for our enemies takes more strength than cursing them does. Preaching to a military congregation about praying for our enemies during times of war is much harder than offering a sermon on the noble virtues of

187

a warrior. Yet this is part of the gospel, a command of Christ, that runs contrary to the values and desires of the world.

But I cannot—*we* cannot—ignore our duty to pray for our enemies. If we do not pray for them, who will? If we harbor only hatred for our enemies, what becomes of our hearts?

Pray for your enemies especially when it confounds you. Double your prayer efforts when such prayer becomes difficult or painful. Triple your efforts when someone close to you is killed in war and you curse the war and those who brought grievous heartache into your life.

Evil cannot be overcome by evil. Only love can overcome evil, and by loving we show that we are children of God.

Pray for your enemies . . . especially when you feel you cannot.

Prayer for Healing Divisions

I have found that there is a common bond in times of great need . . . It is God, who transcends language, faith backgrounds, and strife. Perhaps this recognition is the first and greatest step toward peace. Let us pray together to heal our divisions.

Mighty Creator,
We call you by many different names . . .
We have divided your kingdom into many factions . . .
Worst of all, we have done so in your holy Name.
However, we all turn to you in times of trouble and danger.
We thank you for your mercy and kindness . . .
Hear our prayers . . .
Heal our divisions . . .
Bring us peace.
Amen, amen, and amen.

OUR COUNTRY— PRAYING TOGETHER

In the beginning of the contest with Great Britain,
when we were sensible of danger,
we had daily prayers in this room for Divine protection.
Our prayers, sir, were heard, and they were graciously answered . . .
Have we now forgotten that powerful Friend?
Or do we imagine we no longer need His assistance?
—BENJAMIN FRANKLIN TO THE CONSTITUTIONAL CONGRESS IN 1787

If I had one wish for my country, it would be for us to unite in prayers for peace. It is only a wish . . . a thought . . . unfortunately, a dream. Only when our backs are up against the wall will all of us rally together in prayer. This happened on December 7, 1941. It happened on September 11, 2001. But most of the time between and since, it seems as though we no longer need God's assistance. Benjamin Franklin realized this same pattern just years after America won its independence.

My wish is not for Catholic prayer or Protestant prayer or Jewish prayer or Islamic prayer or any other type of prayer. My wish is simply for us to unite in prayer, in any prayer for peace. Pray as your conscience or faith dictates. Even if only half of us Americans would pray, that would still be 150 million prayers for peace.

God has blessed our nation graciously since its inception in 1776. God has probably blessed us more than we deserve. Franklin asks, and I ask, "Have we now forgotten that powerful Friend?"

You see, I have been all over our amazing nation. I have stood in the observation area in the top of the Gateway Arch in St. Louis. I have stood on Maine's Mount Washington. I have stood in the surf of the Pacific and Atlantic Oceans, the Gulf of Mexico, and the Great Lakes. I have

190

five children, each one born in a different state—Virginia, North Carolina, California, Illinois, and Massachusetts. And I was born in Wisconsin. By my own recollection I have led worship services in twenty-eight of our great states. I have seen the rich blessings that we sing about in songs such as "God Bless America."

At a time when there is so much unrest in the world and when we have troops in harm's way in Afghanistan and Iraq, have we forgotten God's power? Have we forgotten God, who has answered our prayers in the past?

I pray for our country, that we return to our traditions, and that we remember the gracious mercy of God. God will hear our prayers and bless our nation if we repent and unite together. It has happened before; it can happen again.

A nation praying together for peace is a mighty nation, our nation, America!

Another Prayer for Peace

TODAY, WE UTTER NO PRAYER MORE FERVENTLY
THAN THE ANCIENT PRAYER FOR PEACE ON EARTH.
—*Ronald Reagan* [16]

God of All History,
We have studied history,
and there has never been lasting peace.
The history of the Bible is littered with battles and death,
with the conquerors and the vanquished.
Those believing in the myth of redemptive violence
killed even your own Son, Jesus Christ!
Will we ever know peace?
Is the ancient prayer for peace among people possible?
We know all things are possible for you,
O God, but is it possible for humanity?
Can we be saved from ourselves?
We do not know the answer to these questions, so
we have no other choice: we must pray for peace on earth.
Amen.

THESE ARE THE THINGS OF WAR

The point is that war is war no matter how it's perceived.
War has its own reality.
War kills and maims and rips up the land and makes orphans and widows.
These are the things of war.
Any war.
— TIM O'BRIEN, *GOING AFTER CACCIATO* [17]

There are two Green Beans coffee shops at Camp Al Taqaddum, Iraq. Plans are in place to add trailers with Burger King and Pizza Hut. At the Al Asad air base to the northwest, they have these in addition to a Subway trailer. There's also a trailer where soldiers can buy a new Harley Davidson, Chrysler, Ford, or Chevy at a deep discount. These are located near the Beauty and Nail Spa trailer.

Two hours after arriving at TQ, I am on a call at the SSTP when a marine who has been shot twice by a sniper is brought in. He bypasses the emergency room area and is taken straight into surgery. He needs blood, and the call goes out across TQ for his blood type: A positive. I am A positive.

Two hours and fifteen minutes after arriving in Iraq, I am calmly donating blood. Looks are deceiving, though. Inside I am in pieces. A Marine is dying, cut open across his chest and down his abdomen. Blood is filling his abdominal cavity. His aorta is temporarily clamped. It is not good. In fact, it is beyond bad.

I sit up slowly and hold gauze on the place where the needle was inserted into my arm. When I am done donating blood, I am given a T-shirt that says, "I donated blood and saved a life at Camp Al Taqaddum, Iraq, and all I got was this freakin' T-shirt."

Embarrassed, I push the T-shirt into the spacious cargo pocket in my camouflage pants.

193

I hustle back to the operating room. The Catholic priest is there . . . A doctor steps away from the patient and takes off his gloves in quiet resignation. Death is imminent. The once cacophonous sounds and rush of the operating room fade, and the OR is invaded by an eerie silence. It is death.

A shocked friend and fellow marine waits in the passageway of the SSTP. He will volunteer to be a stretcher bearer when the marines of Personnel Retrieval and Processing (PRP) come to pick up the deceased marine.

All the Green Beans coffee, burgers, pizza, motorcycles, cars, and conveniences we add for the troops won't change the realities of a wartime situation. On the first day of my second tour in Iraq, my accommodations may have changed, but on the other side of the wire, just off the base, things haven't changed a bit. Marines, sailors, soldiers, airmen, and Iraqis still die the brutal deaths of war.

I stand quietly and watch as the priest prays over the body of this heroic marine.

I have another year of this duty.

Tim O'Brien is right. War is war no matter how it is perceived. He writes about Vietnam.

This is Iraq. Marines serve with honor. Most go home to see their families again; some won't.

These are the things of war. Any war.

Prayer for Serenity

GOD, GIVE US GRACE TO ACCEPT WITH SERENITY
THE THINGS THAT CANNOT BE CHANGED,
COURAGE TO CHANGE THE THINGS
WHICH SHOULD BE CHANGED,
AND THE WISDOM TO DISTINGUISH
THE ONE FROM THE OTHER.
—*Reinhold Niebuhr, The Serenity Prayer*

Lord,
Remind us that we live under your government first.
Remind us that as Americans,
we live under a democracy second.
Amen.

Lord,
It is not always easy to live under God's rule first.
It is not always easy to place America's rule second.
Amen.

Lord,
We are prepared to pray the Serenity Prayer
during these difficult and perplexing times in our nation.
Grant us serenity, courage, and wisdom to pray
and live with conviction each day.
Amen.

A RECIPE FOR PEACE

1 tsp dried respect
1 cup determination
1¼ tsp friendship
2 truckloads tolerance
1 cup fresh honesty
10 ounces freedom
1 cup love
¼ cup grated serenity
1 tsp protection

I found this recipe hanging on the wall of the hospital at Al Asad air base in western Iraq. It was on a bulletin board of letters sent to soldiers by a fifth-grade class. The author was simply listed as "Irene."

She is a young lady wise beyond her years.

Soldiers in Iraq receive all kinds of artwork by young children and letters from people back home in the United States. Many impromptu memorials drawn by military members appear on the walls of buildings, on posters, and even inside port-a-johns. All of these seem to have two things in common: the desire for peace and the desire to remember those we have lost in war.

Perhaps if we remembered more and prayed more, that would serve as an adequate recipe for peace. Until we do that, we can only hope that Irene grows up and becomes a leader of the next generation.

A Direct Prayer

DON'T BARGAIN WITH GOD. BE DIRECT. ASK FOR WHAT YOU NEED.
THIS IS NOT A CAT-AND-MOUSE, HIDE-AND-SEEK GAME WE'RE IN.
—*Jesus in Luke 11:10 MSG*

God,
You know our thoughts. You know our needs.
You know our desires.
Teach us to pray to you with openness and honesty.
Help us to pray for what is truly important
in our lives and in our world.
Give us perspective to see beyond our own small world.
Grant us courage to believe
that you will answer heartfelt prayer
and that you will use us
to be the answer to others' prayers and emergencies.
Impart to us a thick skin so we can ignore peer pressure and
advertisers and have the time and resources to do your will.

This is a bold laundry list of a prayer, God. We are ordinary
people who know how to speak plainly. Clear up any
confused ideas that we need to pray to you with flowery
language or rambling phrases. Let each of us talk to you
from the core of our being. Life is too important—
our missions on earth are too important—
for us to do otherwise. Hear our courageous prayers.
Enable us to live courageous lives.
Amen.

334 SERVICE MEMBERS

On February 7, 2007, a CH-46 Sea Knight helicopter was shot down outside of Fallujah. The seven marines and sailors killed on board were from this base. I will do anything I can to assist the chaplain as he serves their unit. One of the pilots only had three days left before leaving Iraq. *The Associated Press reports that 334 service members were killed in combat between October 1, 2006 and January 31, 2007.*

I have been on deck, in Iraq, for sixteen days in my second tour, and there have been at least that many deaths in the Al Anbar Province of western Iraq during these first days. *The Associated Press reports that 334 service members were killed in combat.*

Our armor has increased. We are now issued side SAPI plates to enhance our body armor: the plates fill gaps on the sides of our vests. New gel pad systems have been added to Kevlar helmets to make them more comfortable and provide better protection against concussion. Nomex (fireproof) suits and gloves are issued to us before we go outside the wire. *The Associated Press reports that 334 service members were killed.*

I see new vehicles that weren't here ten months ago. Vehicles named Buffalo. Cougars with V-shaped bottoms and better armor to help deflect blasts. I also see interesting multiwheeled rollers that attach to the front of a seven-ton truck to detonate any pressure plate IEDs. Some things change, yet some things remain the same. *334 service members killed.*

Tactics of the insurgency change from pressure plates to command-detonated IEDs. They are also using more explosives in IEDs in an effort to defeat our added armor. And more helicopters are being shot down by small-arms fire.

The Associated Press reports that 334 service members were killed in combat between October 1, 2006, and January 31, 2007. That is more than in any four-month span since the war in Iraq began.

On February 8, a call comes from the SSTP: four urgent surgical cases. Fifteen minutes later the call changes: two urgent surgical cases and two killed in action (KIA). Five minutes later the call changes: one urgent surgical case and three KIA. The last patient does not come to TQ but is taken to Fallujah. He is a recon marine, and I will not know what happened. I know what happened to the other three marines.

While I am at the SSTP, our first sergeant asks me to pray for a friend, Sergeant Major Ellis, KIA near Haditha. He asks me to pray for the marine's wife and daughter too.

Some days it all weighs on you and saps your emotional strength. But I realize that I am not outside the wire, and I pray for those who are and for those who never will be again.

My friends, my marines and sailors, when will enough prayers for peace make a difference?

Powerful Prayer

PRAYER IS SAYING *No*.
PRAYER IS A RESOUNDING *No* TO HELPLESS VICTIMIZATION
ANYTIME, ANYWHERE.
No TO FEAR.
No TO APATHY.
No TO BEING STUCK.
—*Lynne Bundesen*, One Prayer at a Time[18]

All-Powerful Lord,
Hear our prayers of power and might.
Hear us as we thunder with raw emotion and confidence.
Hear us as we claim authority through your Word.
Hear our echoes from the mountaintop.
Hear us when we shout across the waves of the seas.
Hear us roar in the desert.
Hear us from sea to shining sea.
Hear our resounding cries:
Nothing shall separate us from the love of God!
Amen and amen!

POWERFUL PRAYING

*I tell you the truth, if you have faith and do not doubt, not only can you
do what was done to the fig tree, but also you can say to this mountain,
"Go throw yourself into the sea," and it will be done. If you believe,
you will receive whatever you ask for in prayer.*
—MATTHEW 21:21–22 NIV

Prayer is a resounding *No.*" Those words of author Lynne Bundesen precede the selection "Powerful Prayer" for good reason. How many of us believe the words of Jesus quoted above? How many of us practice that type of prayer? When was the last time you said, "No! No!" to those whom you know oppose the will of God . . . "No!" to the fear and worry that accompany your prayer for a loved one at war . . . "No!" to the apathy of others about matters of great importance in your life, your community, and your world? When was the last time you cried out in prayer with a dogged determination and perseverance?

I don't believe enough people pray with such confidence and power.

If more people prayed such powerful prayers, I believe many of the problems we face as individuals, communities, and the world would be solved!

Some of us may go about in a style of false humility and ask God only halfheartedly. Some of us are sincere in our requests but don't really believe that God will answer the prayers of just one person. But I tell you this: a single person praying powerfully, fully expecting God to act, has faith that is contagious. Soon others will join in prayer—in positive and powerful prayer—and soon the mountain will be moved.

The main problem consists of skepticism and lack of faith.

Too many prayers are weak and perfunctory. Sincere, yes, but not very powerful at all. Not nearly faith-full enough to move a mountain. Not even enough to move the person in the pew or chair next to you on Sunday morning.

I ask people to pray for peace all the time, and I know they do. But I am sure that none of them has ever stood up in church to powerfully petition the King of kings for peace. Sure, some may have added the request for peace to the prayer list or stood up during a time of prayer requests and asked for prayers for peace. But I would venture to say that no one has ever demanded it. No one has ever compelled an entire church to pray for peace. And I mean powerful prayer: having prayer meetings for peace . . . contacting other churches to meet together to pray for peace . . . taking out ads in the local newspaper to pray for peace as a community . . . starting a prayer vigil, praying twenty-four hours a day for peace. Do you not remember what Jesus said? "Again, I tell you that if two of you on earth agree about anything you ask for, it will be done for you by my Father in heaven. For where two or three come together in my name, there I am with them" (Matthew 18:19-20 NIV).

Do you know of anyone who is that committed to prayer?

That is the type of prayer that moves people, governments, and the world to action.

It is the powerful prayer that says, "No! No more apathy, fear, victimization! No more fighting!"

That type of prayer requires a powerful, positive, and blinding faith.

That type of prayer can move mountains.

That type of prayer can move people to action.

We have the choice to offer well-intentioned prayers that don't have the power of perseverance behind them, or we can offer prayers that will not accept anything less than the will of God in response.

During times of conflict, can we afford to offer anything other than powerful and life-changing prayer?

No!

So pray like you expect God to answer.

And keep praying.

Then get others to pray with you. Then get even more people to pray with all of you.

PUSH: Pray Until Something Happens!

Pray with unwavering faith.

Pray with power.

And then pray again!

Do you dare to have such a powerful faith?

I can tell you that the men and women on the ground in places like Iraq and Afghanistan need your powerful prayers.

Positive Prayer

WHAT I DO TODAY IS IMPORTANT BECAUSE
I AM EXCHANGING A DAY OF MY LIFE FOR IT.
—*Hugh Mulligan*

My work is important today!
I will do something to further the causes
of freedom, justice, and peace!
I will stand up for those who are oppressed!
I will be the voice of those who cannot be heard!
I will protect those who are in danger!
I will preserve traditions of honor and dignity!
I will contribute to the well-being of my family, friends,
church, community, state, and nation!
I will make a positive difference in the world today!
Lord, grant these requests.
Let my life be bold the same as my prayer—every day!
Amen.

UNDER THE SHADOW OF THE ALMIGHTY

God does not promise a world free of danger. No significant period of history has gone by without one tribe, race, or nation at war with another. This is the unfortunate state of humanity. One can surmise that it will continue to be this way in the future. We hope, pray, and work for peace, but we know that the annals of history do not show us as the peaceful and merciful children God intends us to be.

That is why we live under the shadow of the Almighty. God is our only true refuge and strength. To put our ultimate trust in human hands is to believe that what has happened before does not matter; it is to be ignorant and callous toward the lessons of history.

The writing of these prayers and reflections began with the impending invasion of Iraq in March 2003. At the same time, there were conflicts in Afghanistan, the Balkans, Chechnya, central and western Africa, Tibet, Israel, Palestine, and Kashmir. Against the backdrop of these conflicts, the words of the psalmist in Psalm 91—as ancient as the historic prophets—are as modern as the high-tech weapons used to wage these conflicts.

History will judge the outcome of all these conflicts. In the meantime, individuals and groups will debate the need to defend their lifestyles and physical as well as economic security. In the end, God will judge the hearts of the people involved, and he will judge both their actions and inactions.

With these truths in mind, we can conclude that there can be only one starting place and one ending place for our fallen humanity: prayer. We must ask God to, in his words, "deliver us from evil and save us from the time of trial."

The "war to end all wars" did not end all wars, and this collection of prayers and essays will, sadly, be relevant for years to come. We live in a world wanting peace yet unable to achieve it. So at the same time that we pray for peace, justice, and mercy, we also pray to remember wars and warriors past as well as those who wear uniforms of military service today. It is, to be sure, a constant tension that we cannot seem to avoid.

Two months after returning from Iraq and serving with the SSTP, I know that I will be returning for another year. I am, however, able to spend ten months at home with my family. During this time I revisit the prayers and reflections that I have written. They help prepare me for another tour in Iraq. This time I will be gone for a year. It is what I do for a living. It is what I am proud to do for a living.

If we understand the prophetic words of Psalm 91, we know that no matter where we stand politically on the matters of conflict and war, we still abide under the shadow of the Almighty. And we must pray. I will pray for you. I will pray for your sons and daughters, nieces and nephews, husbands and wives, grandchildren and friends who go in harm's way. First and foremost we will pray together. Praying together is a good first step.

Prayer for Unity

BUT RUTH REPLIED, "DON'T URGE ME TO LEAVE YOU
OR TO TURN BACK FROM YOU.
WHERE YOU GO I WILL GO, AND WHERE YOU STAY I WILL STAY.
YOUR PEOPLE WILL BE MY PEOPLE AND YOUR GOD MY GOD."
—*Ruth 1:16 NIV*

Ever-Faithful Christ,
Bind us together as brothers and sisters, just as Naomi and
Ruth were bound together in love and faithfulness.
Help us to replace "me" with "we."
Fill our lives with commitment, compassion, and generosity.
The assistance of friends helps us
clear the obstacles in our path.
Your aid, O Lord, will make the
mountains lie low and the valleys rise up.
Bind us in unity.
Together our joys will be doubled and our sorrows halved.
Let it be so for today and for all of our tomorrows
until we gather at the feet of God.
Amen.

Prayer in Victory

IN WAR, RESOLUTION;
IN DEFEAT, DEFIANCE;
IN VICTORY, MAGNANIMITY;
IN PEACE, GOODWILL.
—*Winston Churchill*

Gracious God,
In victory we thank you for success and an end to hostilities.
Bring us a lasting peace.
In victory we leave the field of battle as humbled persons.
Having learned the high cost of victory,
we ask you to grant us healing.
In victory we will strive to rebuild the cities of our enemies.
Lasting friends are won with a gracious, helping hand.
In victory we joyously return to our families.
Give them rest under the protection we have provided.
In victory our prayers have been answered.
May we never have times of war again.
Amen.

Prayer of Confession

Lord,
Pardon our inability to live in harmony.
Wars, violence, and coercion have filled our world.
Elevate our spirits so that we can soar above
enmity, strife, retribution, and hatred.
Accept our pleas for forgiveness and renew our respect
for your teachings of grace, mercy, and absolution.
Calm the violence and bloodshed in every corner of the globe
by teaching our leaders the paths of reconciliation.
Enable our children to grow up in a world
that spends its wealth feeding the hungry,
housing the homeless, and curing the sick.
Hear our petitions, O Lord.
Amen, amen, and amen.

PRAYING FOR THOSE BACK HOME

Prayer for the President

Please, Lord, guide our president.
Refresh his spirit as he prays.
Encourage his efforts to make our lives safer.
Send your angels to protect him and his family.
Impart wisdom to him in all of his deliberations.
Deliver unto him judicious counsel.
Empower him to speak with compassion and justice.
Nurture his confidence that you have called him to serve.
Trace his name among the faithful who serve God and country.

Amen.

Prayer for Congress

MAN SOMETIMES THINKS HE'S BEEN ELEVATED
TO BE THE CONTROLLER, THE RULER. BUT HE'S NOT.
HE'S ONLY A PART OF THE WHOLE.
MAN'S JOB IS NOT TO EXPLOIT BUT TO OVERSEE, TO BE A STEWARD.
MAN HAS RESPONSIBILITY, NOT POWER.
—*Oren Lyons, Onondaga faithkeeper* [19]

Establisher of Governments and Nations,
We pray for our Congress. They are leaders of people,
a nation, and the world. Remind them
that great responsibility comes with this power.
Grant each senator wisdom. Grant each representative integrity.
As they meet in sessions filled with
life-impacting decisions, guide their deliberations.
We covenant with you, O Lord, to hold these men and women
in our daily prayers so that together we would
work to make this nation a better place for all people.
Give them respect for you, obedience to your will,
and humility for the awesome tasks and responsibilities
that have been bestowed on them.
And at the close of each day, bless them
with rest and renewal, for a new day lies ahead.
We commend them to your care
and offer this prayer in your most holy Name.
Amen.

NATIONAL PRAYER BREAKFAST

Author and theologian Henri Nouwen once said, "In the end, a life of prayer is a life with open hands where we are not ashamed of our weakness but realize that it is more perfect for us to be led by the Other than to hold everything in our own hands."

Sometimes people debate about whether our nation is blessed by God. Such a question could presume that we are asking for America to be blessed to the exclusion of other nations. But we should all hope our God will bless any nation that humbly requests his blessings. Another presumption is that we are a Christian nation. This is hardly true. We are a nation of people from a variety of faith backgrounds—and some profess to have no faith at all. Thankfully, this does not preclude anyone from praying as he or she wishes.

I believe that the National Prayer Breakfast is a time-honored tradition that seeks to openly recognize that we do not and cannot live without the presence of the Divine. So here are some petitions to pray to God for our nation. One could just as easily change a few words to pray for any nation. As we seek God's blessings for America, we are to remember that we live in a world linked together by economic, political, religious, and a host of other factors. In any case, pray to God for our nation and for all nations. It is a rich tradition well worth the time and effort.

Let us pray:

Gracious Lord, we come before you realizing our need and willing to ask for your help and blessings. We ask you to hear our prayers this morning.

We pray for our Congress: Almighty God, hold each member of Congress in the palm of your hand. Enable them to lead their lives with wisdom and courage. Help them to balance your will and the will of the people in all of their decisions. Be with their staff and their aides who provide crucial support. We ask you to hear our prayers this morning.

We pray for our military: Most Holy Leader, we pray for our military. In these dangerous times, bring calm and peace into the hearts of all who serve. Bless the families who support each service member; bless them in their anxious times. Keep your watchful eye over all who are deployed, and return them safely to their homes. We ask you to hear our prayers this morning.

We pray for our president: Eternal Father, we pray for our president. Grant him discernment as he leads the United States of America. Bring him peace and restfulness here at Camp David. Be with our president and his family, and strengthen their faith. We ask you to hear our prayers this morning.

We pray for our nation: Creator of all nations, we humbly ask your continued blessings on our nation. You have graced us with freedom of religion, abundant harvests, and people willing to serve you and our nation. Indeed, our blessings are too numerous to count. Be with all Americans, and grant them freedom, safety, and contentment. We ask you to hear our prayers.

In the name of the one who is now and forever our Guide, Protector, and Salvation,

Amen.

Prayer for Hectic Times

O WHAT PEACE WE OFTEN FORFEIT,
O WHAT NEEDLESS PAIN WE BEAR,
ALL BECAUSE WE DO NOT CARRY EVERYTHING TO GOD IN PRAYER!
—*Joseph Scriven, "What a Friend We Have in Jesus"*

Dear Lord,
I come to you in prayer today. Life is too hectic,
and I worry that I will not be able to keep up.
I cannot carry all the burdens of work, family, bills,
and responsibilities by myself.
So I turn to you and ask for your help.
If I forget you in the distractions of the day,
I am glad that you do not forget me.
I lean on you as my God, as the Great Listener,
and as my dearest Friend.
I am glad that you are always there when
I call out in either joy or distress.
I know you have many prayers to hear today,
but just this one last thing:
help me to carry everything to you in prayer.
Amen.

I AM THE MARTHA STEWART OF THE FLEET

He's the Martha Stewart of the fleet," I hear one chaplain lean over and whisper to the chaplain seated next to him. I finish my sentence about packing breakables inside a five-gallon plastic bucket and padding them with washcloths and towels. I stop and look over at the two whispering chaplains.

"You're just jealous because I've figured out how to include two pillows, a soccer chair, a 2½ x 4-foot rug, and my soft blankey in my pack-out."

If I'm going to Iraq for a year, you'd better believe I'm going to be comfortable. Some of the comforts of home also include my coffeemaker and coffee, an extra working uniform, and a sweatshirt to wear on cold nights inside the 7 x 15-foot "tin can" that I will occupy for these twelve months. The sweatshirt says "Lenoir-Rhyne Dad," referring to the college my oldest daughter attends. It's not authorized gear, but I don't care.

One of the young religious program specialists (RPs), those soldiers assigned to work with and protect chaplains, gets the idea and says, "I've got to get a couple of those paint buckets. I can put my Xbox inside one of them and all my games and my portable DVD player inside the other." To each his own.

Like every other marine or sailor, I am allowed two seabags (green duffel bags, for you army types) and my pack. Inside of those I must pack all that I need for the year. There is a Base Exchange at Camp Al Taqaddum, but I am leaving in January with $150 that will need to last me until October when I return home for two weeks of R&R leave. So I have gathered my group of chaplains and RPs to show them all the secrets to living

218

in Iraq: sheets (2), blanket (1—soft), fitted sheets (2), mattress cover (1), pillowcases (2), big towels (3) . . . As I go through the list and include health and comfort items as well as military gear, I show them how to use the big 2½-gallon ziplock bags to keep clothes dry. The key is compressing the air out of them to save room.

I'm on a roll: "Make sure you pack your shampoo inside a ziplock bag so that if it leaks, it only leaks into the ziplock. They can throw your bag into a puddle, and when you get to Kuwait, you'll still have dry gear." The big tricks include knowing that one seabag can hold two five-gallon buckets, knowing where to find bigger storage bags that can hold a pillow or blanket, and knowing how to get all the air out of them.

I do cheat a little (and didn't Martha get caught cheating too?) by having a small box of books—professional materials—sent over by the Group Chaplain's Office. A few novels and extra coffee are thrown into my bag for good measure.

My crowning moment is when I ask my fellow chaplains and the RPs how they'll find their own seabag in a pile of hundreds of similar green seabags. I smile and lay my packed seabags on their sides. I have cut a piece of cardboard in the shape of a cross, attached it to the bottom of the seabag, and then spray painted the bottom white. When the paint dries, I remove the cross, and the bottom of my bag is white with a giant, green cross in the middle. Everyone will know who belongs to those seabags: the chaplain. You can pick my bags out of a pile of seabags from twenty yards away.

One RP says, "Cool!" Another chaplain looks at the other and says, "I should've thought of that."

When things get hectic before a deployment, I relieve some of the stress by arranging and rearranging my gear several times until I have it just right. It is then that I realize I am, proudly, the Martha Stewart of the fleet.

I think they're all jealous of my soft blanket. Did I tell you that it has Dale Earnhardt on it?

Remembering Pearl Harbor

YESTERDAY, DECEMBER 7, 1941—A DATE THAT WILL
LIVE IN INFAMY—THE UNITED STATES OF AMERICA
WAS SUDDENLY AND DELIBERATELY ATTACKED.
—*Franklin D. Roosevelt*

Almighty God,
Men slept
Bombs dropped
Ships sank
Americans wept
Never to forget
Funerals held
New resolve
Uphill struggle
Long war
Atoms collided
Victory won
Church bells tolled
Never again
We pray always
Amen.

Prayer on the Anniversary of September 11, 2001

To honor the memories of those who died so suddenly, courageously, and innocently, we will bind together in agreement and prayer with one another. We will bind together on earth so that our prayers and actions will be bound together in heaven.

Let us rise up together, joining hands and bowing heads. Let us pray:

Lord, we wish to bind on this earth the love, compassion,
courage, devotion, selflessness, generosity, and sacrifice that
we have learned from the victims, their family members,
and the responders to September 11. We bind these now.
Lord, we wish to bind on this earth justice, freedom,
equality, and respect for all people of every nation,
language, and race. We bind these now.
Lord, we wish to bind on this earth constant prayer
and outreach to all those who have suffered
in the wake of September 11. We bind these now.
Lord, we wish to bind on this earth prayers for
those who have died to date fighting terrorism,
many of them so far from home. We bind these now.
Lord, we wish to bind on this earth unity and peace.
We bind these now.
Lord, we wish to bind our own prayers
in this moment of silence. We bind these now.
Lord, we thank you for binding these prayers in heaven.
We offer them now to your glory in the memory
of all who died so innocently and heroically in
Pennsylvania, New York, and Washington DC.
So be it and amen.

BOUND BY LOVE AND COMPASSION

Verily I say unto you,
Whatsoever ye shall bind on earth shall be bound in heaven:
and whatsoever ye shall loose on earth shall be loosed in heaven.
—MATTHEW 18:18

Barely moments after the horrific 9/11 attacks, we saw courage, devotion, selflessness, sacrifice, honor, and love rush in to fill the void created by sudden panic and shock.

Minutes after the attack, an able-bodied man would not leave the side of his friend and wheelchair-bound coworker who could not flee the burning tower. While they were binding selflessness and devotion on earth, God bound the same for them in heaven.

At the same time that people fled to save their lives, rescuers rushed to the scene and straight into burning buildings. While they were binding sacrifice and courage on earth, God bound the same for them in heaven.

When death was imminent, people made phone calls, prayed, and took matters into their own hands. While they were binding love, honor, and heroism on earth, God bound the same for them in heaven.

Planes exploded, walls toppled, and towers collapsed. The ground shook, smoke arose, and the world stood still. God cried out, "Greater love hath no man than this, that a man lay down his life for his friends" (John 15:13).

As terrorists expected to celebrate victory, something completely different was loosed on earth. Not terror or broken spirits. No, something radically different was loosed. Americans and friends throughout the world loosed a spirit of caring, compassion, generosity, and determination. Whatever you loose on earth is loosed in heaven. In a matter of days, money poured in—and not a little, but billions of dollars. Blood banks ran out of donation kits, and

222

churches filled to record levels. A spirit was loosed that prompted everything from children collecting pennies to Hollywood stars and corporations donating millions of dollars. New York City churches, like Trinity Episcopal, affectionately known as Trinity on Wall Street, turned their houses of worship into centers to feed and house rescue workers. People with absolutely no connection to the tragedy traveled to the attack sites to volunteer. Construction workers labored around the clock to clear debris, and families came forward with inconceivable strength to share the stories of loved ones they had lost.

Absolutely incredible! It is unlikely that you or I will ever again see an outpouring of the human spirit of that magnitude. I pray to God that we will never need such an outpouring because of tragedy. And so we pray for all who grieve and all who respond in love and compassion. We remember the words of Deuteronomy 15:11: "Thou shalt open thine hand wide unto thy brother, to thy poor, and to thy needy, in thy land."

Morning Prayer

DO NOT PRAY FOR EASY LIVES. PRAY TO BE STRONGER MEN.
DO NOT PRAY FOR TASKS EQUAL TO YOUR POWERS.
PRAY FOR POWERS EQUAL TO YOUR TASKS.
—*Phillips Brooks*

O God,
For this new day we give thanks.
We ask for:
Stamina
Faithfulness
Hope
Wisdom
Power
We promise:
Loyalty
Respect
Commitment
Creativity
Exuberance
With your unfailing support,
our efforts and accomplishments are unlimited.
We work together to glorify you and our country today.
Amen.

Evening Prayer

THE REWARD OF A THING WELL DONE IS TO HAVE DONE IT.
—*Ralph Waldo Emerson*

Most Blessed God,
As we bring this evening to a close,
we thank you for the physical and mental ability
to work hard and honor you. There is glory and
there is peace in our labors. We have risen to every challenge
of the day and performed in a manner that
reflects credit to God, country, family, and self.
Be with those who stand the watch tonight as we
sleep under the blanket of freedom that they provide. Grant us
rest from our labors so that we might awaken refreshed to live,
work, and honor you yet another day.
We end this day as we began: in prayer and
with thanks to you, our Redeemer and Protector.
Amen.

ECHOING THE PRAYERS OF THE SAINTS

REMEMBER THE SABBATH TO KEEP IT HOLY

It was still Saturday in North Carolina when 243 marines and sailors boarded a DC-10 bound for Kuwait. We arrived at Hahn Air Base near Frankfurt, Germany, on Sunday afternoon for a seven-hour layover. We reached the final destination of Kuwait City just as time expired on Sunday. Two Navy chaplains were embedded with these units from the 2nd Marine Logistics Group, one Protestant and one Roman Catholic. Those are the cold facts.

The real story is that, as with all other deploying units, there is a mixture of sadness about leaving family and friends and a sense of excitement about the mission and the adventure of a year in Iraq. Souls of warriors are vulnerable, caught in limbo between home and Iraq and laying over in Germany on a crisp, sunny afternoon. Seven hours of discussions, books, cards, iPods, DVDs, and naps. Layovers are generally a pain in the neck, unless . . .

It is the Sabbath. Remember the Sabbath? Or perhaps you might phrase it as a command: Remember the Sabbath! Two hundred forty-three marines and sailors are secluded in a passenger terminal on the Sabbath. One Protestant chaplain and one Roman Catholic chaplain are in the mix. One is a fourteen-year member of the Chaplain Corps and a veteran of Operation Iraqi Freedom; the other is in his first year in the Navy, and this is his first deployment. The two are together on the Sabbath and ready for the first challenge.

Now, that setting is a dream for any pair of chaplains. In all honesty, there was no worship service planned. We were supposed to be at Camp Virginia in Kuwait, where there's a great ministry to all service members transiting in and out of Iraq. But when opportunity presents itself, there flows the Holy Spirit and a chance to worship.

An opening prayer, a reading from Luke 7:1–9, a short sermon, prayer requests, and a closing prayer with a blessing . . . A group of fifty-plus worshippers met by the TV in the nonsmoking lounge of Hahn Air Base on a Sunday on their way to Iraq. After this ecumenical gathering, Father Jose Bautista, the Catholic priest, held a liturgy of the Word for the twenty or so Catholic parishioners present.

Navy chaplains exist for these moments—these times when the sacrifice of dedicated marines and sailors draws them away from the ability to worship with their families and friends at home. Marines and sailors go in harm's way. Chaplains deploy with their troops every day of the week. No matter where we are on the Sabbath, it is holy. And it is the sacred duty and honor of chaplains to provide holy moments and pathways to God, wherever the Marine Corps sends us.

Worship was offered, spirits were lifted, and two Navy chaplains began forming a strong bond with their marines, their sailors, and their God. There is no better way to start a yearlong deployment in support of Operation Iraqi Freedom.

Ooo-rah—and amen.

The Lord's Prayer

Our Father which art in heaven,
hallowed be thy name.
Thy kingdom come,
thy will be done in earth,
as it is in heaven.
Give us this day our daily bread.
And forgive us our debts,
as we forgive our debtors.
And lead us not into temptation,
but deliver us from evil:
For thine is the kingdom, and the power,
and the glory, for ever.
Amen.
(MATTHEW 6:9–13)

PRAYING IN TIMES OF CONFLICT: A CONSTANT NEED

Operation Iraqi Freedom, Joint Endeavor, and Desert Storm have been major military operations since my birth in 1961. We're very careful not to use the word *war*. We have "operations," "conflicts," and "humanitarian aid missions." The word *war* is generally reserved for conflagrations of an immense magnitude.

So threatened was the United States after the attacks of September 11, 2001, that the ensuing campaign was named the "Global War on Terror." So we are at war now. But if we include "operations"—of which more than eighty occurred during the 1990s alone, both at home and abroad —we can see that our country has been in constant conflict my entire life. And if you don't think that military operations count as conflict, just check with a military member who has come under fire during one of these operations. In my lifetime, conflicts and operations have killed people by the hundreds of thousands in Cambodia, central Africa, the Balkans, and Asia. Armed conflict is a condition of humanity. And so we must pray!

Are my prayers needed—and do they make a difference?

Absolutely! An eighteen-year-old woman marries her high school sweetheart while he is on leave after graduating from infantry school. The idealistic couple sets off from their small Midwestern hometown, hoping that the U-Haul towing their compact car will survive the trip all the way to their new home just outside of the main gates at Camp Lejeune, North Carolina. Two months after setting up housekeeping, the husband—a lance corporal in the United States Marine Corps—is sent with his unit to the front lines of battle. A network of Marine Corps Key Wives is in place to help the new bride cope with the sudden separation and the fears that are part of the life of a military member's spouse. Still, nights are long and incredibly lonely. Not knowing the day-to-day fate of her husband is the source of the young woman's greatest fear. If her husband is going to make a career of service to the Marine Corps, she will quickly learn that this battle will not be his last. She will learn that in recent years marines have come under fire in Liberia, Kosovo, Afghanistan, and Iraq. Some of these places she previously could not even pick out on a world map. The young wife and her husband are in constant need of support whether we are officially at war or not. Prayer will become a constant companion of the spouse and the marine.

Whether the country is at war or engaged in a humanitarian operation, all families associated with military service have a constant need for support and prayer. We have to pray constantly for peace. We have to pray constantly for an end to the human sin of conflict. Individuals and governments have tried unsuccessfully for generations to end human wars and conflicts. Prayer is the only thing that can make a difference. And so we must pray. And so we will pray: Our Father which art in heaven, hallowed be thy name. Thy kingdom come. Thy will be done in earth, as it is in heaven. Give us this day our daily bread. And forgive us our debts, as we forgive our debtors. And lead us not into temptation, but deliver us from evil. For thine is the kingdom, and the power, and the glory, for ever. Amen.

Prayer Attributed to St. Francis of Assisi

Lord, make us instruments of your peace.
Where there is hatred, let us sow love;
Where there is injury, pardon;
Where there is discord, union;
Where there is doubt, faith;
Where there is despair, hope;
Where there is darkness, light;
Where there is sadness, joy.
Grant that we may not so much seek
To be consoled as to console;
To be understood as to understand;
To be loved as to love.
For it is in giving that we receive;
It is in pardoning that we are pardoned;
And it is in dying that we are born to eternal life.

Psalm 23

The LORD is my shepherd; I shall not want.
He maketh me to lie down in green pastures:
he leadeth me beside the still waters.
He restoreth my soul:
he leadeth me in the paths of righteousness for his name's sake.
Yea, though I walk through the valley of the shadow of death,
I will fear no evil: for thou art with me;
thy rod and thy staff they comfort me.
Thou preparest a table before me
in the presence of mine enemies:
thou anointest my head with oil;
my cup runneth over.
Surely goodness and mercy shall follow me
all the days of my life:
and I will dwell in the house of the LORD for ever.

A TIMELY WITNESS

He said to them: "It is not for you to know the times or dates the Father has set by his own authority. But you will receive power when the Holy Spirit comes on you; and you will be my witnesses."
—ACTS 1:7–8 NIV

This was the text for one particular Sunday sermon. Five minutes into the sermon, I heard the radios of the doctors present in the congregation crackle with the word of an incoming patient with a gunshot wound to the neck. Not good. But the pulpit is my place on Sundays even when a call comes in for a surgical case.

I was preaching about time—about living on God's time and not on our time. Military folks probably understand this concept better than civilians. The time we spend deployed is time with our family and friends we will never get back. And, even more so, we do not know the times or dates that God has set for each of us who lives with imminent danger. The sermon was one that would ring true with everyone in attendance.

After speaking with the marines, soldiers, sailors, and civilians as they left church, I heard the phone ring and knew that one of the religious program specialists would answer the call. It was the SSTP asking for a chaplain "right away." With that, I grabbed my hat and literally ran over to the SSTP.

Fear turned into reality: the victim of the gunshot wound was a young marine. My place was now to minister to the crew of the SSTP and offer a prayer for the deceased. I thought immediately of the verses spoken of during the sermon: "It is not for you to know the times or dates the Father has set . . ."

Against this backdrop of death, a surprise awaited me at the SSTP. A young corpsman came up to me and quietly said, "Did you see his PPE?" I

236

hadn't looked at the marine's personal protective equipment. His flak jacket had been cut away in order to get to his wounds. As it had fallen to the floor, the back SAPI plate (the small arms protective inserts inside the "bullet-proof" vest) had slipped from the Velcro enclosure of the vest. The corpsman took me over and showed me the SAPI. Taped to this marine's SAPI was a copy of the entire 23rd Psalm. I looked down and read the familiar words: "Yea, though I walk through the valley of the shadow of death, I shall fear no evil . . ."

Tears clouded my eyes, yet a smile came across my face as I nodded in acceptance.

So now I am finishing this sermon for me and for all of you who read this. I am finishing it in memory of a fallen marine who became a timely witness. The beginning of Acts 1:8 (NIV) says this: "But you will receive power when the Holy Spirit comes on you; and you will be my witnesses."

The 23rd Psalm for Sailors

The Lord is my Skipper,
I shall not drift.
He guides me across the dark waters.
He steers me through the channels.
He keeps my log.
Yea, though I sail amidst the tempest of the sea,
I shall keep my wits about me.
His strength is my shelter.
He prepareth a quiet harbor before me.
Surely the sun and the stars shall guide me
and I will come to rest in heaven's port forever.
—HOMER HICKAM, *THE KEEPER'S SON* [20]

Psalm 46

God is our refuge and strength, a very present help in trouble.
Therefore will not we fear, though the earth be removed,
and though the mountains be carried into the midst of the sea;
though the waters therof roar and be troubled,
though the mountains shake with the swelling therof.
There is a river, the streams whereof
shall make glad the city of God,
the holy place of the tabernacles of the most High.
God is in the midst of her; she shall not be moved:
God shall help her, and that right early.
The heathen raged, the kingdoms were moved:
he uttered his voice, the earth melted.
The LORD of hosts is with us;
the God of Jacob is our refuge Selah.
Come, behold the works of the LORD,
what desolations he hath made in the earth.
He maketh wars to cease unto the end of the earth;
he breaketh the bow, and cutteth the spear in sunder;
he burneth the chariot in fire.
Be still, and know that I am God:
I will be exalted among the heathen,
I will be exalted in the earth.
The LORD of hosts is with us; the God of Jacob is our refuge.

CAN WE LIVE WITH PEACE?

We look forward to the time when the Power of Love will replace
the Love of Power. Then will our world know the blessings of peace.
—WILLIAM GLADSTONE (1809–1898)

I am a pilgrim, a wanderer.
I shall remain a wanderer until mankind has learned the way of peace,
walking until I am given shelter and fasting until I am given food.
—PEACE PILGRIM

Each day we pray for peace in Iraq. I just hope that it arrives in Iraq soon. And when I say "soon," I mean in the next three to five years (that is, unfortunately, soon in light of the present reality). Otherwise there will be an entire generation here in Iraq that does not know peace.

Then what will they teach their children?

There will be a generation of distrust.

There will be a generation of fear.

An entire generation will have been lost to a war of random violence.

A war of IEDs . . .

Improvised Explosive Devices . . .

Indiscriminate, Excessive Death.

So I am left to wonder if the people of Iraq will know how to live with peace. Will they be able to live without a sense of fear or numbness? Will they, after a dictator and a war, know what to tell their grandchildren about how to live life?

Or will their stories be about how to survive life?

Even my children. Will I be able to explain to them that one of the ribbons I wear on my military uniform is called the "Global War on Terrorism Ribbon"? Does it mean that there is no peace worldwide? Does it mean that people and politicians cannot, with all of their reasoning and learning, co-exist in our world?

I hope and pray that we can live with peace. I hope and pray that I can have hope for the future. In my forty-five years on this earth, there has been the Global War on Terror, Desert Storm, the Balkans, Rwanda, Vietnam, apartheid, the PLO, the IRA, troops still in Korea—the list is too long to continue. And all of this in less than half a century . . .

I wonder . . . can we live in peace?

I pray that one day we will have the chance.

Psalm 91

He that dwelleth in the secret place of the most High
shall abide under the shadow of the Almighty.
I will say of the LORD,
He is my refuge and my fortress:
my God; in him will I trust.
Surely he shall deliver thee from the snare of the fowler,
and from the noisome pestilence.
He shall cover thee with his feathers,
and under his wings shalt thou trust:
his truth shall be thy shield and buckler.
Thou shalt not be afraid for the terror by night;
nor for the arrow that flieth by day;
nor for the pestilence that walketh in darkness;
nor for the destruction that wasteth at noonday.

A thousand shall fall at thy side,
and ten thousand at thy right hand;
but it shall not come nigh thee.
Only with thine eyes shalt thou behold
and see the reward of the wicked.

Because thou hast made the LORD, which is my refuge,
even the most High, thy habitation;
there shall no evil befall thee,
neither shall any plague come nigh thy dwelling.

For he shall give his angels charge over thee,
to keep thee in all thy ways.
They shall bear thee up in their hands,
lest thou dash thy foot against a stone.
Thou shalt tread upon the lion and adder:
the young lion and the dragon shalt thou trample under feet.

Because he hath set his love upon me,
therefore will I deliver him:
I will set him on high, because he hath known my name.
He shall call upon me, and I will answer him:
I will be with him in trouble;
I will deliver him, and honour him.
With long life will I satisfy him,
and show him my salvation.

THE 91ST PSALM

God often reinforces certain themes in our lives. In early 2003, as it became apparent that we were headed to war, I began a prayer book that would be distributed to the congregation at Camp David, the presidential retreat where I was stationed. The underlying theme of the booklet was the 91st Psalm. The booklet was entitled *Under the Shadow of the Almighty*. In my own search for what to say to this unique congregation, I took comfort and inspiration under the shadow of the Almighty.

Two and a half years later—and just two months after finishing my tour at Camp David—I am deployed with the Marine Corps to western Iraq. Again I find myself seeking God's will during a very stressful time. When I came to the Al Asad air base, I came across this story:

A story coming out of World War I indicates that the 91st Infantry Brigade of the US Expeditionary Army was preparing to enter combat in Europe. Most of them were "green soldiers" who had never seen combat duty. Its commander, a devout Christian, called an assembly of his men where he gave each a little card on which was printed the 91st Psalm. They agreed to recite the Soldier's Psalm daily.

The 91st Brigade was engaged in three of the bloodiest battles in World War I: Chateau Thierry, Belle Wood, and the Argonne. While other American units similarly engaged had up to ninety percent casualties, the 91st Brigade did not suffer a single combat related casualty.[21]

244

I realize that, whether I am in the luxurious confines of Camp David or in the blistering hot sands of Iraq, I am still—and always will be—under the shadow of the Almighty.

So now, when I pray with convoys before they head off on a mission, I lead them by reading the 91st Psalm. Their missions are filled with land mines, rocket and mortar fire, and small-arms fire. Convoys request the presence of a chaplain before they leave, and they expect prayers to accompany each mission briefing. When I lead worship services in Iraq, I always include a reading of the 91st Psalm. The marines, sailors, soldiers, and airmen present realize the need to live under the shadow of the Almighty. I hope and pray to see them again in a few days or on the next Sunday when the cycle begins again.

Until then, we all live under the shadow of the Almighty.

AFTERWORD

Throughout the events leading up to the war in Iraq and during the war, God has answered countless prayers, and I have found that his answers often come from those people around us. A prayer by an anxious spouse is answered when another spouse who has gone through the same anxieties of war comes alongside. A prayer for healing is answered by a medic, corpsman, nurse, or doctor. A prayer for safety is answered by a marine or soldier who stands post through the dark hours of the night. A prayer for comfort is answered by dozens of churches, organizations, and individuals who send care packages almost every single day.

It is a very real fact that we human beings have been at war throughout our entire history. War has proved to bring out the very best and most heroic of humanity while simultaneously exposing what can only be described as pure evil. This is the price we pay for the great freedom of will that God has given us.

No matter what your thoughts are on this war or any other, I urge you to pray continually for those who go in harm's way and for those who govern us and make the decisions that send our troops around the globe.

War has drawn me closer to God. My spiritual life is heightened as I depend on God to get me through each day. The prayers and reflections that you have just read are merely a few of those that I have written. As a chaplain with sailors, marines, coastguardsmen, soldiers, and airmen, I have written daily prayers for almost five years straight. I shared those prayers via e-mail, entitled "Prayers from Catoctin Mountain" and "Prayers from the Sands of Iraq," with those I have been stationed with during my two tours for

Operation Iraqi Freedom. The prayers are a part of what can be called "prayer and social engagement." I believe that we should be forthright with God about our concerns, hopes, and praises. Never is there such a time to be socially engaged than when our security is threatened and we are seeking peace.

In reality, daily prayer helps keep me focused on God's love and grace, for his love and grace have made it possible for me to serve in such diametrically opposed places as Camp David and Camp Al Taqaddum, Iraq. If you use some of these prayers and reflections in your daily walk, I will be humbled as God's messenger.

Your prayers for the troops and your support of them mean more than you will ever know. The war on terror may be with us for some time just as wars have been a constant in our history. Pray for peace; pray for understanding; pray for wisdom . . . Whatever you do, keep praying.

ACKNOWLEDGMENTS

To God be all glory and honor. The care and wisdom of the Almighty has made this work and my life possible. I am awestruck every day that God chooses me to be a messenger of the Word.

There is no way to adequately thank my wife of twenty-one years, Leigh, for her love and support. She is why we have such wonderful children. Mariah, Janie, Megan, Will, and Erin—you all make me smile and laugh each day. For twenty months while I was in Iraq, you went without a husband and father. This is time we'll never recover. You serve our country the same as I do. I love you all.

This book is not possible without the significant help of two wonderful authors. The first is Lynne Bundesen, who is a mentor and teacher. Many of these prayers and stories were done on a computer she sent after the insurgency blew mine up with a rocket attack! Thanks so much. The second author is one of America's premier storytellers, Homer Hickam. More importantly, he's a Vietnam veteran who knows the importance of the stories of our nation and military. Thanks so much for your continued support and getting me to my agent, Frank Weimann at the Literary Group International. Thanks, Frank, for your quick actions on a timely subject—and to his assistant, Elyse Tanzillo, who was always right there to answer my questions.

The team at Thomas Nelson has been nothing short of marvelous! Thanks to my editors, Matt Baugher and Jennifer McNeil, who've given this so much of their heart and time. Add to that Emily Sweeney and her team of marketing and sales folks, who got this into your hands, and

ACKNOWLEDGMENTS

Stephanie Newton, publicist, whose words and enthusiasm bring out the importance of this book. Writing a book, it turns out, is the easy part. Without this team my book is merely a file on my computer.

Special thanks to the marines and medical team with the Second Marine Logistics Group, the crew at Camp David and every other assignment I've held. I've had the honor to serve with some incredible men and women. Our military is filled with everyday heroes who spend the best years of their lives working long, dangerous hours. To serve as a chaplain to these people is humbling. It is with great respect that I thank all who've ever endeavored to serve our nation.

NOTES

1. "President Bush Addresses the Nation," The Oval Office, 19 March 2003. http://www.whitehouse.gov/news/releases/2003/03/20030319-17.html.

2. Gen. Douglas MacArthur's speech to the Corps of Cadets at the U.S. Military Academy at West Point, N.Y., May 12, 1962, in accepting the Thayer Award.

3. Herman Melville, *Redburn, His First Voyage*, ©1849.

4. Martin Luther King, Jr., speech, Detroit, Michigan, June 23, 1963.

5. Harry Chapin, "The Cat's in the Cradle," © 1999 by Harry Chapin. Rhino Records/Warner Chappell Music/ASCAP. All rights reserved.

6. John Barlow Jarvis, Naomi Judd, Paul L. Overstreet, "Love Can Build a Bridge," © 1990 by John Barlow Jarvis, Naomi Judd, and Paul Overstreet. Universal Music/ ASCAP. All rights reserved.

7. Scott Stapp and Mark Tremonti, "Arms Wide Open," © 2000 by Scott Stapp and Mark Tremonti. Dwight Frye Music Inc. and Tremonti Stapp Music/BMI. All rights reserved.

8. Billy Ray and Cindy Cyrus, "Some Gave All," © 1992 by Billy Ray and Cindy Cyrus. Sly Dog Publishing Co. and Universal Songs of Polygram International Inc./BMI/ASCAP. All rights reserved.

9. Gen. Douglas MacArthur's speech to the Corps of Cadets at the U.S. Military Academy at West Point, N.Y., May 12, 1962, in accepting the Thayer Award.

10. President John F. Kennedy. Remarks to the graduating class of the U.S. Military Academy, West Point, June 6, 1962.

11. Eric Clapton and Will Jennings, "Tears in Heaven," © 1992 by Eric Clapton and Will Jennings. Blue Sky Rider Songs and Warner Chappell Music/ BMI. All rights reserved.

12. *Braveheart*. Written by Randall Wallace, produced and directed by Mel Gibson. © 1995. Paramount Pictures and 20th Century Fox. All rights reserved.

13. President Dwight D. Eisenhower, in "The Chance for Peace," a speech given to the American Society of Newspaper Editors on April 16, 1953.

14. John F. Kennedy, 22 November 1963, address to the annual meeting of the Dallas Citizens Council, Dallas, Texas.

15. Homer Hickam, *We Are Not Afraid* (Deerfield Beach, FL: Health Communications, Inc., 2002). Used by permission.

16. Ronald Reagan, Second Inaugural Address, 21 January 1985.

17. Tim O'Brien, *Going After Cacciato* (New York: Broadway Books, a divison of Random House, 1978).

18. Lynne Bundesen, *One Prayer at a Time* (New York: Touchstone, a division of Simon & Schuster, 1996).

19. Steve Wall and Harvey Arden, and edited by White Deer of Autuum, *Wisdomkeepers—Meetings with Native American Spiritual Elders* (Beyond Words Publishing, Inc., 1990), 64.

20. Homer Hickam, *The Keeper's Son* (New York: St. Martin's Press, 2004). Used by permission.

21. Michael and Brenda Pink, *Psalm 91: The Ultimate Shield for Enduring Protection* (Nashville: Thomas Nelson, 2001).